Our Spiritual Companions

Adam Bittleston

Our Spiritual Companions

From Angels and Archangels to
Cherubim and Seraphim

Floris Books

First published in 1980 by Floris Books, Edinburgh
Fifth impression 2004

British Library CIP Data available

ISBN 0-86315-433-6

Printed in Great Britain
by Cromwell Press, Trowbridge

Contents

Acknowledgement

Unless otherwise stated, all quotations from the Bible are from the Revised Standard Version with kind permission of the National Council of Churches of Christ. (New Testament © 1946, 1971; Old Testament © 1952.)

Introduction

If we listen for such things, we often encounter people who have had experiences at some period of their lives which go beyond the range of the familiar senses. They may have known themselves outside their physical bodies, they have had dreams which left the impression of a meeting with reality otherwise unknown to them, they have felt the presence and help of a friend or relative who has died. Often these experiences have been disturbing and they may find it difficult to speak about them. And yet it may be evident that such moments have had a strong influence on their lives.

Our civilization has no place for such things, or only, if they become very disturbing, some treatment for psychiatric illness. Particularly among young people who have not yet found a definite place for themselves in the world, devastating problems can develop in this way. There is a great need for people who can hear about unusual experiences without emotion or hasty judgment. We need a more general recognition that there are worlds all about us for which there are no accepted maps. Maps have indeed always existed, though not in the sense of lines on paper — and were there long before the continents and oceans of earth were mapped. We have forgotten them; and shall not find them or make them afresh, until the need is felt deeply enough.

Something else has happened, though very incompletely. In the universe as conceived by the astronomer today there is no reason why there should not be millions of planets with life on them, though our immediate neighbours seem rather inhospitable. And many of them could have had intelligent beings on them for much longer than the earth has. Why then have we no evidence of superior intelligences, with technologies much more advanced then ours, communicating with us and perhaps giving us the benefit of their advice? There is indeed a feeling that there may be holes in this conjecture; yet it is not unreasonable, given the picture of the universe that exists today. It can be carried a few steps further; we may ask what really superior intelligences would think about our civilization. Perhaps they might disapprove of it—so we may feel uneasily. Perhaps they might ask whether we want them to communicate with us; and whether it would be good for us if they did.

It is often forgotten how short a time it is since most people on earth *were* sure that superior intelligences existed, communicated with us, and gave us the benefit of their advice. Great changes in the mind are gradual, and the evidence for them many-sided. Taking for the moment only that part of Europe lying west of Poland and Hungary, perhaps it can be said that in 1450 most people believed that angels guarded and guided human beings, and that by 1700 very many did not. Fifteenth-century European painters and sculptors represented angels with warmth and conviction; eighteenth century artists, with the exception of William Blake, hardly ever did. It would be difficult to get much good advice from a baroque marble angel.

Through the loss of belief in the angelic hierarchies both the idea of God and the idea of man suffered change. Without the perspective given by conceiving rank upon rank of spiritual beings, from the Angels to the Seraphim, it became possible to think of God much more egotistically and self-righteously, as a personal adviser, entitling one to disapprove of everyone else. By the end of the seventeenth century this had already happened on a terrible scale. And man could think of himself as God's favoured creature, the only other intelligent being.

About the same time, perhaps earlier, human consciousness was impoverished in another way as well. All those beings vanished away completely, who had been felt as peopling the woods and streams, just beyond the range of our eyes and ears, and not to be counted or measured by human minds. The elemental beings are relegated to poetic fantasy and it is quickly forgotten that ordinary people had believed in them and indeed known them well. And yet it is only the heads of men that really reject them, the senses and the brain that say they are not there. In our feelings and in our will we are still with them, sometimes comforted and sometimes mocked, an increasing riddle to ourselves. First in our houses and cities, then even in the fields and woods, we miss them, and do not even recall their names much less their forms. It had always been hard to represent, outwardly or in the mind, beings so constant in their change.

Around the turn of the fifteenth to sixteenth century there were some outstanding assertions about the reality of the heavenly hierarchies and the elemental beings. Most of them were not much noticed, or were even held back by the people who made them; the climate of opinion was changing quickly against them.

Then there came a witness who was heard, and is heard everywhere today. But he was not, and is not, taken as a witness about spiritual realities. For Shakespeare, man is always surrounded by the angels, the elementals and the dead — whether he knows it or not. It is not only in *A Midsummer Night's Dream* or on Prospero's island that nature is abundantly peopled by spirits. Man in his need is always being led into places where the trees have voices and the streams bring comfort and wisdom; whether in Wales or on the coast of Bohemia or by the temple of Diana at Ephesus. In this book, Shakespeare will be quoted much more than any other English writer. His greatness may appear to have very little to do with the angelic hierarchies — but this greatness has its roots in his sense of man's dependence upon a universe of living beings. Nowhere else in English literature do we find an imaginative creativity so much in harmony with the creative work of the nine hierarchies, made manifest in nature and in human destinies. Of course this cannot be proved; but it is one of the purposes of this book to show how such a conclusion may be reached.

We do not often find the names of the hierarchies in Shakespeare, though they were deeply felt and understood by a Londoner, John Colet, only a few years before his time. Colet was Dean of St Paul's, a great preacher, learned in the history of Christianity and deeply concerned about the critical spiritual situation of his time. He knew well, and wrote a heartfelt commentary on, *The Celestial Hierarchies*, attributed to Dionysius the Areopagite, the pupil of St Paul. This and other writings attributed to Dionysius had enjoyed great authority for nearly a thousand years, deeply influencing such men as John Scotus Erigena, Thomas Aquinas and Dante — but in Colet's time were beginning to be discredited, the Italian scholar Lorenzo Valla having maintained that they must have been written much later than the first century. It is now generally agreed that they originated in the first half of the sixth century or thereabouts. But their intrinsic value stands; and they may well be linked by a continuous esoteric tradition with the school of St Paul at Athens.

When Dionysius or Colet write about the hierarchies, it is as if they were describing tremendously honoured friends. They are awed, but their love overcomes their awe so that they dare to write. And as priests, they were doing what was expected of them, if they spoke of God and his angels. It was not expected of a London playwright under Elizabeth. Indeed, great trouble was likely to come from the Puritan civic authorities of London. Shakespeare generally avoids both the name of God and the name of Christ. But he had just the same sense of the nearness of the spiritual world that was possessed by John Colet or by Thomas More, or in his own time by the charitable and sensitive theologian, Richard Hooker. Shakespeare knew too that contact with the spiritual world can bring great difficulties. Those who are not aware of contact with the spirit may easily grow impatient about Hamlet's uncertainty; was the vision of his

10

father's ghost sent by heaven or by hell, or perhaps from a place in between? For many people today it is a real and very painful problem — how should they regard something that has seemed like contact with someone who has died, perhaps bringing burdens or temptations with it. The need to learn something about the environment of the dead may then become compelling.

For Shakespeare, both the living and the dead are following paths which lead through purification towards maturity. The souls of men, in either state, may ascend in contemplation from the Angels to the Throne of God. To speak with these beings, or to speak about them here on earth, will always be a struggle with words. It is part of Shakespeare's extraordinary achievement that he always makes it apparent, for anyone who listens carefully enough, where any of his characters stands upon the inner path. It very soon becomes evident, for example, what degree of self-knowledge a man or woman possesses. In *Twelfth Night* Sir Toby Belch and Sir Andrew Aguecheek have a splendidly complete absence of self-knowledge; in Malvolio it is grotesquely distorted through his relationship to a private god he calls Jupiter. In Sebastian it shines out bravely; not only in the sense of knowing one's own limitations, but in a recognition of the tension in which all human beings live. He is thought to have been drowned; and when he reappears, he is thought to be a ghost. He declares:

A spirit I am indeed:
But am in that dimension grossly clad
Which from the womb I did participate.[1]

Full self-knowledge has to encompass both the eternal individuality and the circumstances into which it is born on earth. We are born into a particular social position, and it has often been said that Shakespeare regards it as disastrous if the order of rank in society is disturbed. This view comes to expression most vividly in the famous speech of Ulysses in *Troilus and Cressida*:

11

> Take but degree away, untune that string,
> And, hark! what discord follows.[2]

Ulysses describes a chain of being, extending from the stars through human society to all nature; everything with its right movement and function. This was a familiar medieval view: and this order of stars, men and nature was felt as reflecting, though imperfectly, the order of the hierarchies. But Shakespeare does not take what might be called the simple conservative view. A man or woman may not be born in that place in society where he or she ought to stay. Everything depends upon the motives behind a desire for change. Macbeth and Coriolanus speak in voices harsh with ambition; Helena, the physician's daughter in *All's Well that Ends Well*, seeks nobility from a clear and profound resolve. A human being who seeks change may be guided by his Angel or be defying him. Wherever a human being comes to stand receiving or seizing responsibility or divesting himself of it there will always be those above him and those below him.

There is a far-reaching difficulty here. Can we bear it, to have a particular place, to fit into some category? Can we bear not to? Is everything in the universe — if it is good — just receiving and carrying out orders from above? Where the path of spiritual development has been fully understood, it has never been regarded just as a path of obedience. It is a growth into freedom as well as an awakening to the will of the spiritual world. Both belong to maturity; and on the way there has to be a reconciliation with one's place in the world, and with one's own unique individuality and fate. Shakespeare describes this struggle, which can be bitter, in one of his sonnets:

> When in disgrace with fortune and men's eyes
> I all alone beweep my outcast state,
> And trouble deaf heaven with my bootless cries,
> And look upon myself, and curse my fate,
> Wishing me like to one more rich in hope,

Featur'd like him, like him with friends possessed,
Desiring this man's art, and that man's scope,
With what I most enjoy contented least;
Yet in these thoughts myself almost despising,
Haply I think on thee, — and then my state,
Like to the lark at break of day arising
From sullen earth, sings hymns at heaven's gate;
For thy sweet love remember'd such wealth brings
That then I scorn to change my state with kings.[3]

Feeling himself loving and loved, Shakespeare can accept both his outer status as a playwright (no great thing) and his inner condition, that of one with sufferings and insights which separate him from others.

But is the problem of freedom and obedience really solved in this way? It has by no means been solved by humanity in general, up to our time. We have dismissed angels and kings, and finally God himself, not to have anything or anyone above us. In every large or small social unit, the problem of any kind of authority is acute. We are trying to get rid of every kind of hierarchy on earth; is it thinkable that we should again accept heavenly hierarchies? The problem is a real one, not just a matter of moral theory. It has to be solved in real relationships.

It can help us to see that the scattered witnesses to the spiritual hierarchies from Shakespeare up to our own time are by no means unfree people but show considerable freedom both towards outer convention and towards their own world of vision. To Swedenborg, William Blake, Goethe, the world of angels is just as real as the human world; but they make their own decisions. And we may see that they bear out Shakespeare's indication — the problem is to be solved through love.

And now in our time a great curtain has been drawn back. While still in his thirties, Rudolf Steiner described what freedom is within the human soul — how it comes about and how it is made effective — more clearly and thoroughly than

13

any other philosopher. He shows that the human being need not follow any advice, or obey any commandment — but will grow to his full stature in fulfilling those pictures of action which his moral imagination can create for itself. *The Philosophy of Freedom* was published in 1894. From 1900 onwards Rudolf Steiner began to speak about the beings and events of the spiritual worlds, from his own perception of them. His accounts were on the surface matter-of-fact and undramatic: but they gradually built up an immensely rich and many-sided picture of the universe. It was never closed, never completed: as questions were answered, new and greater questions opened up. But the nine heavenly hierarchies, as Dionysius had written of them, were there again; and now they were shown to be at work, not only as messengers between the Godhead and man, not only in never-ceasing worship and praise, but also as receiving special tasks in bringing about the evolution of the cosmos, the earth, and humanity. Rudolf Steiner could describe these beings as he did, because he met them. Such meetings were for him just as certain and definite as meetings with another human being. This was only possible because he had passed through the most earnest work of self-knowledge, and could stand before these beings without pride or fear.

In the use of the names of God and Christ, Rudolf Steiner was very sparing; but he was quite consistent from 1900 until his death in 1925, in showing how the contemplation of nature, history, and the spiritual hierarchies could lead to a deepened understanding of Christianity. In the last eight years of his life he returned again and again to the Temple of man's physical body as a revelation of Father, Son and Holy Spirit. He showed that modern man needs this recognition very deeply, both in the ordering of his social life and on his journey into his own inner being.

When he spoke of the spiritual hierarchies, Rudolf Steiner was often concerned to show that they provided the environment for the souls of men between death and a new birth. Of course the beings of the spiritual world are

14

countless and of many, many kinds; but the recognition of the Third, Second and First Hierarchies is as fundamental there as our understanding of the differences between stone, growing plant, and animal is here. Whether we are dealing with stone, plant and animal, or with other human beings, we try to understand something about the other's history. With a garden flower for example, it is good when we are cultivating it, to understand something about the wild varieties. With the human being, it can be very helpful to know to what school he or she went, or whether his or her early childhood was happy or not. It may seem very strange to some if it is said that something of the same kind applies to the angelic hierarchies. It belongs to the essence of their being that they have cosmic memories, as we remember our earthly lives. Of course, even with other human beings if, for example, they describe their early childhood to us, our power to imagine what it was like for them is limited; and we can hope at the most to make only tentative beginnings in understanding those mighty realms of experience to which a spiritual being can look back. But particularly in his *Occult Science — An Outline* and in many other places as well, Rudolf Steiner has given far-reaching help in this direction. At some points in these chapters on the hierarchies we shall need to look back at earlier conditions of the universe as described by Rudolf Steiner; and only a very concentrated summary of these can be given here. Nobody to whom such descriptions are unfamiliar is asked simply to accept them; the words in which they have to be described are indeed so inadequate that an immediate acceptance would be of much less value than a willingness to suspend judgment until their meaning grows.

Much in our present universe is predictable; the movements of the planets for example, in relation to sun and earth, can be calculated within very close limits. Countless processes on earth, both in the living and in the lifeless, go on in a predictable way. We tend to take this for granted, and indeed are inclined to regard our failures to predict many things in advance as due simply to defects in our knowledge. Now one way to describe a world which is so calculable would be to say: we live in a winter universe, the world has frozen into law. Inwardly we grow cold if we contemplate this regularity alone and do not feel the presence of any spontaneity anywhere around us. Were we not to recognize free creative activity, most evidently in other human beings, the winter would seem unbroken.

But it was not always so. Rudolf Steiner describes a universe, not linked with ours by any continuous chain of physical causality, in which was manifest everywhere the free creative power of spiritual beings. It was a spring-like universe, a world of fresh beginnings: Rudolf Steiner describes something that is very difficult for us to imagine — that of what are traditionally described as the four elements, fire, air, water and earth — there was only fire. If a being, equipped with our present physical senses and nothing more, had visited this primeval universe, he would have observed only varying conditions of warmth. But qualitatively this warmth would have had all the promise and wonder that we find in the present universe where things begin — for instance in very young living creatures. To this ancient universe, for reasons which need not be considered here, Rudolf Steiner gives the name, Old Saturn.

The universe which followed Old Saturn, and is called Old Sun, was a summer world, filled with light, abundance and beauty. When this had passed away, another universe came into being, which can be compared with what we know in our present world in temperate regions, as autumn; a time of storm. While on the Old Sun, light, warmth and air existed, on this third universe, Old Moon, there were also what corresponded to our watery or fluid element and the forces that underlie what we know as chemical processes. In this world we can think of moods of alternating grief and hope, of a struggle from dream towards wakefulness. Thus the sequence leads to our present world with its solid substances and calculable events that yet contains, wintry

16

though it is, its own promise in the development of full, conscious freedom. In this whole mighty process the beings of the hierarchies are concerned; and to have some feeling for their part in it is helpful in our relationship to them, just as it may be helpful, when we meet another human being, to know something of the joys and sorrows and responsibilities in her or his past life.

If we on earth develop a clear and lively feeling for the spiritual hierarchies, this can strengthen the relationship between the living and the dead. It is our great task after death to find a right relationship to the beings above who serve the Good: it is not achieved all at once. The puzzling moods and impressions experienced by many people have often to do with this. As on earth, so after death, questions are not always answered at once; the effort to find an answer, the effort to learn, has a value in itself. For those who have died the external circumstances of those they have left behind are generally much less important that the extent to which those on earth grow to maturity.

The dead look into our pain, into our sorrow, into our sense of failure; they watch what happens in us, as we can watch movements in a landscape. They see how in us acceptance of destiny and creative freedom are continually meeting; and they can be comforted by the kinship between their tasks and ours. If we begin to look towards the hierarchies with comprehension for their significance in our lives, we breathe with the dead a common light.

We meet on earth what we see as evil. We are learning to accept that improvements in the social order, better education and so on (things very valuable in themselves) will not eradicate violence and crime. These have much deeper roots. Evil is to be found in the spiritual world as well; and this too can be expressed in troubling spiritual impressions, particularly among young people and even children. Certain drugs too can bring, along with very different impressions, openings into hell appallingly real and lasting in their effects. Even to be much occupied with evil actions in recent or

17

earlier history can exert a kind of fascination, and lastingly disturb the mind's inner balance. Yet we do need to face the fact of evil, not just theoretically, but with all our capacities of mind and soul.

> There is some soul of goodness in things evil,
> Would men observingly distil it out . . .[4]

but this distillation has to be done in the presence of much immediate, straightforward goodness. We need to look long at the Archangels who praise God and serve him without ceasing, before we are ready to consider what happens when an Archangel goes wrong. This expression is of course, like most of our words applied to spiritual things, a kind of uneasy metaphor; and yet what has happened has always been described in some such way. Lucifer is only to be understood as a noble and yet fallen spirit.

Man is to redeem the spirits of evil not through blind obedience to the good, but through the exercise of a freedom which has indeed a wakeful and perceiving obedience in it, but also contains entirely new creative deeds.

The relationship between the greater and the less in the universe is not such that the greater simply commands the lesser being. The greater may reveal a purpose which the lesser can receive in devoted reverence, and make its own in action. But the greater can also be utterly silent, and wait.

The Third
Hierarchy

1. The Angels

Of the nine hierarchies, the Angels are nearest to the soul of man. Yet in our age we are very little aware of their presence and their work. This is not only because we are in general so unaware of spiritual beings; it is in the nature of the Angels not to draw attention to themselves. They are the guardians of individual human beings. Through a whole series of its incarnations, they accept the task of watching over a particular soul. But their field of vision is not limited to the thoughts and feelings of this one soul, though these are very significant for them. They do not see physical objects as we do; they look on beings, and the relationship of beings. Into their own souls there sound and sing the voices of the higher hierarchies, giving them purposefulness and hope. Each night they encounter the soul of the one who is their special concern, and seek to remind him of his own deepest purposes. We are often caught up in problems which are a matter of hours or days; our Angels have always before them years and lifetimes.

In waking life, we are likely to achieve some consciousness of the Angel's presence when we try to understand events in our own lives separated from the present by months or years, or when in prayer we ask for help most earnestly. At such moments the Angel tells us that our lives as a whole have a meaning, and that we are being watched over, and protected. What seem to be great misfortunes may indeed befall us, or we may do great wrongs to others; but every event will in the end reveal its positive sense.

For the Angel has both a powerful, far-reaching memory of the past, and a lively relationship to the future. His memory reaches back, indeed, to a universe that existed before anything which we can see on earth or in the sky; a universe in which there was much yearning and grief, in which the Angels shared, when their consciousness was much more like our own present consciousness. When today we meet other human beings, we can sometimes come to know that they have led a childhood in which there were times of acute unhappiness, which influenced them deeply, though they may have grown into strong and happy people, achieving much in the world. Something comparable, on an immensely greater scale, has happened to the Angels.

On Old Moon, human beings were still sunk in dream, while the Angels grew into responsibility. But now the Angels see how human beings are growing into knowledge of the universe around them, and of each other; at first indeed a knowledge of objects, and a relatively superficial understanding of people, but before long into an awakening knowledge of the spirits of the universe, to be achieved while we are still dwelling in the earthly body. St John's Gospel records that the Christ said to his disciples: 'you will know the truth, and the truth will make you free'[5]. This promise for man lives in the hearts of the Angels: St John's Gospel as a whole is indeed written in their language, and composed for their understanding.

In quite specific ways too the Angel feels the approach of the future. During earthly life, individual human beings are generally very little aware of when and how death will come to them. The Angel is much more aware, and in a quite different way, of the significance of death. Often his delicate warnings are concerned with this. For example, somebody we know may be near to death, and we do not realize it; but the Angel would like us to say something to him, or write something to him, while he is still on earth. Or there may be something important to be done, before we ourselves die. The Angel is immensely careful — speaking in rather human terms — not to intrude upon our freedom with such warning. But we may have grown sensitive enough to observe that a thought or feeling, which it would be quite natural for us to have, shines in our minds with a radiance and intensity a little greater than is usual, and calls us to action a little more insistently. We are still quite free to respond to such a call, or to neglect it.

The Angel himself is not born, nor does he die. But the births and deaths of the one committed to his charge are times of very great significance for him. Before birth, the Angels are among the last spiritual beings on whom souls can look. They may carry over into childhood a mood of thankfulness for this patient, watchful care, which may then be identified with what is done by the mother, or other loving people. But a child may even at times see its own Angel, or feel its presence strongly. The Angel is watching with deep concern how far the earthly body is going to provide a fit instrument for the purposes which the soul has carried with it from the heights of the spiritual world. All sorts of hindrances are threatening these. They may be endangered even during pregnancy by the thoughts and feelings of the mother. The delicate senses of the new-born child may receive harmful shocks. The Angel is concerned that the child should sleep away as it were, those impressions of earth which are not helpful to it. In this the Angel is not alone. A kind of community of Angels comes about as Botticelli has painted it in his *Nativity*, the Angel of the child seeking to work with the Angel of the mother and those of others truly concerned, including the Angels of brothers and sisters, whether these are on earth or to be born later. In our time, there may be special difficulties in the achievement of co-operation between the grown people concerned with the development of a child, for instance between father and mother or between teacher and parents. The Angel of the child may then have to work in a special way to make good what goes wrong here.

As the child grows up, the Angel may seek an opportunity to give him or her some inkling of the character of previous earthly lives. In conflicts and uncertainties, it may be of great importance for the human being to feel: there are certain positive aims which have guided my existence on

22

earth again and again in the past, and which I shall find afresh, when I achieve a certain tranquillity of mind. There are periods of history, and perhaps groups of people, among which I can recognize, looking back through time, the warm radiance of these aims. But I can also recognize certain deeply engrained weaknesses in myself, which have hindered the fulfilment of these aims in the past, and may do so again.

There are considerable dangers at this point, especially if it seems that a particular historical individuality is being indicated. Innumerable people, for instance, have believed themselves the reincarnation of Mary Magdalene or Judas. This need not be just a crude mistake. There may really be some quality of soul present in one who has such a belief, a quality fittingly pictured in this way. Perhaps nearly everyone can find a Judas in himself. For certainty about the connection of individualities much more is needed than cloudy intimations or even extensive clairvoyant powers.

Even the thought that a particular individuality may be one's former incarnation may seriously threaten an inner balance. A man may, for example, to some extent fall in love with himself; he may come to feel that he has a genius within him, which others ought to recognize. If this happens the contact with his true Angel is likely to be broken or weakened, and a Luciferic spirit, a proud Angel, may draw near to him. The hard experience of many years may be needed to put this right. On the other hand, delicate indications given by the true Angel may be received in deep quietness and humility, and be fruitful over many years.

When the human being passes through death, it is generally not easy for him, especially if he has a long life on earth behind him, to perceive at once the form of his Angel, and establish a relationship with him. Some of his strong attachments to earth existence must first be purified, and he must learn to regard his past life with understanding. It is as if his Angel, and other beings of the hierarchies, were behind him, drawing his attention to certain events of his past life on which he can look, and come to comprehend in their effects on others. Gradually the content of his nightly meetings with his Angel, received then in almost entire unconsciousness, will awaken within him. He will come to recognize the Angel as the source of wise guidance about the consequences of his past life, not only for the earth, but for the spiritual world into which he is entering. Not much more than a hundred years ago such thoughts as these were quite familiar to the Gaelic-speaking people of the west of Scotland. Alexander Carmichael (1832–1912), a civil servant concerned with taxation, wrote down, in Gaelic, verses from the lips of crofters, and translated them into English. One such set of verses described how the Guardian Angel is charged by the Father God to lead a soul in sleep into the company of the holy ones, as a shepherd leads a sheep into the fold.

> Thou angel of God who hast charge of me
> From the dear Father of mercifulness,
> The shepherding kind of the fold of the saints
> To make round about me this night;
>
> Drive from me every temptation and danger,
> Surround me on the sea of unrighteousness,
> And in the narrows, crooks and straits,
> Keep thou my coracle, keep it always.
>
> Be thou a bright flame before me,
> Be thou a guiding star above me,
> Be thou a smooth path before me,
> And be a kindly shepherd behind me,
> Today, tonight, and for ever.
>
> I am tired and I a stranger.
> Lead thou me to the land of angels:
> For me it is time to go home
> To the court of Christ, to the peace of heaven.[6]

Elsewhere Alexander Carmichael records that it was held that a bad soul was led during sleep to a place from which he could catch a glimpse of hell.

Not long after the publication of Carmichael's first volume of *Carmina Gadelica*, in 1900, a German poet, Christian Morgenstern (1871–1914), who himself possessed an angelic gentleness and tranquillity, wrote lines as profound and almost as simple:

O if thou knewest how thy countenance
Is changed, when in the midst
Of that pure gaze which can unite thee with me
Thy hold upon thyself is lost
And thou dost turn away.
Just as a landscape in clear light
May suddenly cloud over, thou dost close
Thyself against me, and I have to wait
And wait in silence, often long.
And if I were like thee a human being
Neglected love would kill me.
But since the Father gave me endless patience
I wait for thee unshaken
When it may be thou comest.
Even this hesitant reproach
Be no reproach — only a quiet sign.

*   *   *

How can we strengthen, in the course of life on earth, our connection with our own Angel? Everything that is done in tranquil prayer or meditation is a contribution to this. And we do a great deal to overcome barriers between ourselves and the Angels if we try to quieten in ourselves feelings of anger, or envy, or even irritation. But there is a teaching which can in a quite special way draw our attention to the things that have to be done in order to help on from our side the building of a bridge between Angels and men. This is

25

Buddha's teaching of the Eightfold Path. The Buddha proclaimed this Path as the remedy for all that has brought suffering to humanity—ignorance, and the desire which springs from ignorance, and all the attachment to the world of the senses in which this desire is manifested. The Path is composed of eight far-reaching endeavours: towards the achievement of right conceptions, right resolves, right speech, right action, right livelihood, right aspiration, right recollection and right contemplation. (In different accounts of the Path in English, varying words are used; none can entirely cover what is meant.)

Through the faults and weaknesses of earlier lives, each man carries within himself much that darkens his understanding and infects his desires. So he brings suffering on others and on himself. Through the practice of the Middle Way, the Eightfold Path, he begins to bring his destiny into order. He begins to be concerned with his task in the same way as his Angel is concerned. There are of course dangers here of self-centredness and a sort of esoteric priggishness, but the Path truly followed constantly leads us *out* of ourselves into the world. Right conceptions are knowledge of the world, right resolves are service to the world, right speech is what others can truly hear, and so through all the eight endeavours. The darkening of understanding confined us within ourselves, the infection of our desires made us aggressive and self-seeking; the Path lets in the light.

The description of the Path which follows is of course very inadequate and very incomplete. It is undertaken from one particular point of view; that we may see a little more clearly how the Path leads towards harmony with the intentions of the Guardian Angel. It is not a question here of describing the Path as it was understood in the earliest centuries of Buddhism, but of how it can live today in those of every faith, because they can find it within themselves, from early childhood onwards, if they look deeply enough.

We live in the glorious variety of experience brought to us by the senses. But this experience is always something that is

26

incomplete. We have to think, in order to find how forms and colours, sounds and tastes, are related to one another and to the beings of whom they are manifestations. As we think, we use concepts of many kinds; for example straightness, causality, goodness, consistency, of which many seem to have an evident relationship to the experience of the senses, while others seem more remote. But if we observe carefully, we can notice that we have to bring them from another part of our being, to meet what is given by the senses, and interpret it. We may for example be awakened by a noise, and feel it echoing on in us, and yet be unable to attach any concept to it. We then might say 'I do not know what it was'. Or, to take a much more significant example, we may observe astonishing or perhaps distressing actions done by someone whom we thought we knew well; and we have to recognize that our conception of him was inadequate. At the beginning of the Path, we are called to observe the concepts we use very carefully, and see how far they enabled us to understand the world truly. And we shall have to return again and again to this point; we shall have to ask of many ideas which have long been ours, whether they are really helpful, whether they are growing in clarity, whether they are consistent with other ideas which are significant for us.

We can never simply *have* right conceptions. We have to grow in them, they have to grow in us. The Angel contemplates the life of thought within the soul. He sees where we are in error, or one-sided in our thinking. But he cannot intervene directly. He may be able to indicate, in the most unassertive ways, that we should pay more attention to phenomena which do not fit in with our firmly established ideas. He can help us to feel the qualities and ultimate effects of different ways of thinking. He can strengthen for us the basic sense for truth. And his whole existence as Angel will be deeply influenced by our progress or lack of progress in this realm.

In order to form any great or small resolve, we need the right conceptions. But on the other hand, someone may feel

27

himself the possessor of an abundance of good ideas, and yet seem incapable of making the smallest decision. An idea has to be related to our conception of our own being, and then go through something like a process of incarnation, putting on warmth and life, before it becomes a full resolve.

Even the smallest resolve we make has its place in our lives as a whole. To get up in the morning, to eat breakfast, to go out of the house — all these can serve in the fulfilment of resolves which extend over years. On the other hand, what seems to us quite a minor decision may lead us away from essential things to be done. Deep within ourselves, we may feel at certain moments: for this I was born. And at other times: what I am doing now estranges me from my fundamental concerns. But whether we feel these things or not, the Angel knows where our resolves are leading. He can compare them with the intentions we have gathered in the spiritual world before we were born. He stands in awe before the mysterious process by which a spiritual idea becomes incarnate in earthly action.

The third endeavour on the Eightfold Path is for right speech. Human beings are called to watch over everything they say. Their right conceptions and their right resolves must give form to their words. Not conventional attitudes of mind, but what each one really thinks, what each one really intends, is to be expressed.

Buddhist tradition points to four dangers into which our words can fall. They are untruthfulness, the desire to wound, slander, and triviality. Untruthfulness is something much wider than intentional lying. If one is asked the way, and with an eager desire to help sends someone off with inaccurate instructions — this is nevertheless untruthful. And it enters speech in much subtler ways. In the course of reminiscence, details may be heightened; or the impression may be conveyed that the speaker has much greater knowledge of the subject than he really has; or he may talk in such a way that his hearers do not really understand him. In all these ways and in many others, one may wander off the Path.

The desire to wound may take hold of a man's soul — or it may be present in a mood of quite short-lived irritation. Generally it springs from a sense of being unfairly treated in some way; to the speaker, what he says often seems a reasonable counter-attack. The effects may be far-reaching. One wounding sentence may be remembered over years, when everything else said by the person concerned has been forgotten. Such things have lasting effects because they in some way attack the deepest concerns of the hearer. They imply that he is not achieving and perhaps can never achieve the purposes for which he came to earth. Hamlet, when he 'speaks daggers' in effect tells his mother that her relationship to his father, and her relationship to him, have been utter failures. A handicapped young woman said, 'I was told I would never be able to work. It wasn't true.' Another young woman was told that she would never make a teacher; over many years, she proved this mistaken. Hamlet and the advisers of these two women may well have thought what they were saying to be true and necessary; indeed, similar things may sometimes have to be said. But the speaker should always ask himself very earnestly: have I to say this — or could what has to be said be put in a more acceptable and more positive form?

People or things are slandered when they are spoken of in such a way that their image is diminished in the minds of the hearers. Generally slander is thought to apply only to people; but if wasps are described as horrible creatures or squirrels said to be 'only a kind of rat' (as in Walter de la Mare's deeply ironical poem) then wasps, squirrels and rats are being slandered. All 'reductionism', all 'this is only . . .' belongs here: 'birdsong is only a claim to territory', 'the rainbow is only an optical illusion'. It may be objected that an image has often to be diminished in the interests of truth. But our image of a living person or thing is never really too great, though it may be too simple or too one-sided. A man loved by a woman is generally seen by her as better or more gifted than he is; but what she is seeing is not a fiction but the real ideal of manhood through him, beyond him.

Since the Angels are constantly receiving into their being in profound reverence, the voices of the hierarchies above them, they experience a most terrible contrast when they observe human speech as wounding or slanderous. It is as if a man were to see a green landscape he loves enveloped in a great fire or afterwards blackened or frozen in a dark fog. Like patient foresters or farmers the Angels seek to restore what has been destroyed. They can only do this where human beings are willing to contribute their part by the cultivation of reverence.

Finally, why is speech so often trivial? Words can do so much good, and can do so much harm; in trivial, conventional speech they do little of either. We may take refuge in it to avoid the responsibility of having a real effect. Perhaps the source of triviality in speech is ultimately lack of courage. We are not prepared to show ourselves, or to find others. We tone down all the powers of speech, like the colours on Newton's disc, into uniform greyness.

Trivial speech restricts itself to a very small vocabulary, because it is anxious not to surprise the hearer in any way, but to reassure him that the speaker is as ordinary as he can be. Cliché calls to cliché, without the slightest effort. It is all very comfortable; but the river of speech trickles away into desert sands. To be silent witness of this is thirsty work for the Angels. For them each word is a living creature, with a great history, and promise for the future. And here a few of them are being idly used, and the rest ignored. He who walks the Path has to feel his share in the downfall of words and he can hope that they may be consecrated once more, in the light of true, developing conceptions and through the life of courageous resolves.

The fourth endeavour of the Path is to achieve right action. What has been understood and resolved within the soul, what has been spoken about with others, is to be carried out into external fact. It has to encounter what proceeds from the thoughts and intentions of others. Conversation can

30

easily become argument; different opinions can exist side by side, but different acts — they try to occupy the same space, and come into collision.

A familiar and on the whole encouraging example of this problem is the driving of a car. We resolve to go from A to B. But on the way a great number of decisions have to be made; these often involve a choice between entering a certain space and giving way to another user of the road. Fortunately the rules are easily understood and generally respected; though they call for a certain alertness. But in life as a whole, we often have to make rules for ourselves, or decide in a particular situation on its own merits. The Path calls on us to avoid conflict, or any kind of destructive action, wherever we can. We are to find room for the fulfilment of our resolve without denying space to others. As in driving a car, we have to be quick to see where others intend to go.

Since the time of the Buddha, external life has become very much more complicated. A man's place in society was then generally decided by his birth; and the fifth endeavour of the Path, right livelihood, called him to fulfil with understanding and devotion a task already allotted to him, as Arjuna was called to fulfil his task as a warrior. Today a man or woman may occupy in a lifetime four or five, or even twenty or thirty, very different jobs. And these may all be of his or her own choosing. Some may have been left because they did not seem to provide a right livelihood at all, but to be causing pollution of the spiritual or physical environment; others, out of longing for a more satisfying work or because a new stage of life had been reached. Everywhere problems come up; what is the relationship, for instance, between a person's capacities and the work he is doing? Is he under continual strain, or is too little being asked of him? How do he and his fellow-workers regard each other?

As has been said the Angels see not things, but beings and the relationships of beings; not machines, but what men do with them. The Angel contemplates, with an infinitely subtle gaze, how life is aided, and how it is destroyed. He sees, for example, the part played by iron in human civilization. It has been very much used and continues to be used, in weapons and armaments of many kinds, for the assertion of power over territories. It has an affinity (as many turns of speech testify) with the quality of aggressive self-assertion in man. In various forms as steel it achieves great hardness. Man learnt its use as he himself grew harder inwardly. In a wonderful rune of the *Kalevala* it is described how when smelting was being learned for the first time the smith intended to mix into the iron a little honey; but through a misfortune what entered the iron was a hornet's sting. Ever since, iron has been quick to wound.

The Angel sees how often an iron stubbornness enters into human action and human work. At some stage of its existence, every human soul has to learn self-assertion; but only that he may sacrifice it again, in service to others. He must keep the achievements of iron in his soul, but refine them, and temper them with honey; and he himself must become mercurial, capable of changing to meet the changing needs of those around him. The Angels are deeply heedful of the transition from the virtues of iron to the virtues of mercury — or from Mars to Mercury in the celestial language — in human action and human work. Pioneers in industry, for example, have often possessed the iron virtues in abundance; but sooner or later, in every business and indeed every community, mercurial virtues prove themselves to be needed above all. And at some point in his life almost every individual has to learn this transition, at least in part; from possessiveness to sharing, from competition to co-operation, from participation in conflict to participation in healing.

The sixth and seventh endeavours of the Path are concerned with a self-education which learns to look in the right way into the future and back into the past. (Here some differences of emphasis from the Buddhist tradition may be noticed.) Anyone who understands himself even a little notices his limitations — the many things he cannot do, the kinds of beauty to which he does not respond, the realms of knowledge in which he has no share. And often these limitations are regarded as absolute and conclusive. 'I shall never understand mathematics'. 'He is quite hopeless with machinery.' 'Bach means nothing to us.' On the other hand, there is something in human nature which rebels, quite rightly, against being condemned to such limitations for ever. Nothing that human beings can do, or love, or understand can be absolutely alien for any of us; in each one, manhood in its universality is hidden.

In our time, there are special possibilities for people of every age to develop new capacities. The use of a new language, the practice of a new art may be taken up late in life, and bring great joy. Every such endeavour brings us nearer to a sense for humanity as a whole, beyond the limitations of the immediate environment in which we grew up. Something like this is often very significant in religious life as well; we grow into understanding for a different faith, or for a religious tradition which had remained alien to us. At such moments of discovery, the future lights up for us. Some things may indeed be unattainable in this incarnation; but as Lessing said, 'Is not eternity mine?'

There is a being who bears an Angel's form, but is greater than all the Angels. Once he bore a human form, as Christ Jesus, and shows the effects of earthly life and earthly death, as the Angels in general do not. When in our time an earthly man grows towards sharing in the development and the aspirations of humanity as a whole, transcending with humility some of his own limitations, his own Guardian Angel can see how he comes nearer to the Angel in whom the Christ Spirit lives.

If during life on earth we were able to look back into the past with the full insight which we may develop after death, we would see that we have incurred much more moral debt to others than we can pay back during this incarnation. Without knowing this clearly, human beings — especially in later life — often feel their memories burdensome. There

33

may indeed be certain moments or periods which we can hardly bear to remember at all. As has been described, the Guardian Angel is going to lead us step by step into a positive understanding of all that has happened. But the Angels alone could not prevent human memories from falling sick in the present time, and more and more so in coming centuries. For the healing of memory the help of Christ is needed. We had seemed to be enclosed in our own memories alone, from a certain point in childhood onwards; but we begin to see each personal life as only part of a vast landscape — and over there, nearly two thousand years away, is the hill of Golgotha. Yet across this great distance of time the strength comes from the place of the Cross, which enables us to accept all the weaknesses and blunders we can recognize in the life behind us, and to make positive use of them.

The eighth endeavour of the Path draws together all the preceding seven. In moments of quietness, we are to see without emotion what has been achieved and what has not been achieved, in the light of our understanding of life as a whole. We are to listen in tranquil devotion to the speech of the world around us, and find our true selves in response to this speech.

It is a difficult problem, especially for Buddhists in the West: Who is it who really goes on the Path? The Buddha teaches that the self, as we experience it in our ordinary consciousness, is a complete illusion. But who else can we find to make all the necessary decisions in the following of the Path? How can this lonely, irritable, aggressive self in us even be able to recognize what right speech is, for example, or control us in such a way that we begin to make it our own?

In reality there is a self belonging to each of us which is not to be found with the ordinary consciousness, but has a hidden existence; it is this self which the Angel tries to guard, and to reveal to us at certain moments. The Path is the work of this self in the ordinary consciousness. As we grow in understanding for the hierarchies above us, the everyday self changes. It learns to be servant, not unruly lord in the house of earth.

34

2. The Archangels

In tranquillity, the human soul can feel itself as if in the shade of trees beside a mountain stream. Anxieties and impatient wishes fall away; the water sings with a low and gentle voice, which unites with the voice of memory, recalling events which bring comfort and hope.

Presently the traveller stirs and decides to go on with his journey. The path leads out on to steep grassy slopes, mounting steadily. The sunlight is strong, but not harsh. The traveller comes without halting to the peak of the mountain, looking out everywhere through the limitless air. And now another voice speaks to him; it is warm and triumphant, awakening in the traveller courage and endurance. Now he is concerned with events that reach far beyond the limits of his own life, great events which have been and others which will come. He feels as if he could write prophetic lines, and bring them down into the village to which he is going.

In the differences of mood between the bank of the stream and the mountain top we have something which may be compared to the difference between the presence of the Angels and the presence of the Archangels. But it must be remembered that the Angels, through their great selflessness, are always bringing to humanity impulses from the realm of the Archangels and from still higher spirits. The Archangel is to the Angel like a brother who can remember very much further into the past, a past of great nobility and splendour of which he often tells his younger brother. In a family we often echo each other's voices unintentionally; the Angel consciously takes into his voice some of the power of the Archangel.

As the Angel gazes upon the development of an individual

soul, the Archangel indwells the development of a nation. But just as a man may look at an event as one of his successes, while the Angel may see it as a misfortune, distracting him from his real task — so what seems a victory to the people of a nation may be a spiritual defeat for its Archangel. What he wants for his nation is not power, but ways of life which serve the great purposes of humanity. He works above all among the artists, the thinkers and the reformers among his people — who may of course be engaged in active protest against many of that nation's policies. Just as a man's pride in his own genius is a great hindrance to his Angel, national pride blocks the work of the Archangel, produces indeed an appalling caricature of it. Human beings do not support the spirit of their country by trying to be French, or Italian, or English, but by working for justice, or the freedom of the oppressed, or beauty in the arts and in the environment. The Archangel wishes to see what is achieved or hoped for by individuals pass over into general habits and customs which enrich life.

The character of an Archangel — or perhaps of several — is deeply impressed into the language of a people. Changes go on continuously in the sounds, meanings, and uses of words. A change may be short-lived, like a fashion which prevails for a few years and is then forgotten; or enduring. The Archangel, working deep in our feelings about language, may have made his choice. It is wonderful to observe, for example, how a word may be taken over from one language into another; it may retain the qualities of the language from which it has come, so that a slight effort has to be made in speaking it. Many French phrases retain this quality in English. Or the word may be so thoroughly assimilated that its origin is forgotten, that it sounds and looks as if it were part of the language which has received it. But a language may also quite quickly reject a word that has belonged to it for centuries, or change the meaning of a word of its own quite radically. Through countless changes of this kind a language is differentiated from its neighbours. But the process cannot be understood as much more than a host of random accidents until it can be seen as the work of a spirit, just as we find the work of his spirit in a man's changing behaviour. Yet there is a deep puzzle bound up with this. Over the face of the earth, men use such different sounds for what appear to be the same meanings. And we understand only a handful at best of the languages which are spoken. The Angels have been described as leading men out of conflict into agreement. Could the greater spirits, the Archangels, be responsible for what seems such a source of division, the variety of languages?

A dictionary is never entirely truthful, when it puts words of different languages as having the same meaning. In living speech the meanings of words are continually fluctuating, even when spoken by the same person. But a word in a particular language has for its speakers in general a host of relationships and implications which are not identical with the apparently corresponding word in another language. Take 'truth', *'vérité'*, and *'Wahrheit'*.

Even with words for what seem to be quite simple objects or ideas the shades of meanings which belong to them may be very different, though they are dictionary equivalents. It may take pages to explain in English the use of a small Greek preposition.

If human beings were more transparent for one another, we would look straight through a sentence our neighbour speaks, in whatever language it might be, and experience all the shades of meaning he intended. But our powers of hearing are dulled. This is the Babel of which the Bible speaks. Not that language is differentiated, but that tongues other than our own have become babble in our ears. 'Babel' means 'The Door of God'; through the Archangels the power, the love, and the wisdom of God could enter the words of men. But when men tried to build towers into the heavens (instead of climbing up a proper mountain) their understanding for each other fell. Yet the greatest works in any language reach out beyond its frontiers and when they are devotedly translated, enrich the language into which they come.

For the English language, the most outstanding example of service to the Archangel in the realm of speech is the work of Shakespeare. The English vocabulary is an extraordinary compound of words of Germanic origin and words coming from Latin. The Latin words always tend to overburden it, like a knight wearing too heavy a suit of armour. Sometimes they have even yet not been completely assimilated. Shakespeare always uses such words — except, of course, when he is mocking pedantry — in a way that warms and enlivens them.

> Shall I compare thee to a summer's day?
> Thou art more lovely and more temperate.[7]

The two words of Latin origin, 'compare' and 'temperate', have nothing burdensome about them, because of the simple words among which they stand and the musical echo between them. Examples of this are everywhere to be found in the plays and the sonnets. Monosyllables with varied vowel sounds and repeated consonants prepare for some magnificent word, which comes in like a prince among courtiers who have awaited him.

> Nor did I wonder at the lily's white,
> Nor praise the deep vermilion in the rose: . . .[8]

Shakespeare did his work with an exceptional selflessness which is not always observed. His own griefs and sorrows are very well hidden; generally they have to be guessed at rather than seen. The one place where he seems to speak directly of his troubles is in the Sonnets; though it must be remembered that a sonnet sequence is a work of art, not a fragment of autobiography. Yet who can really doubt that the voice which speaks with such humbleness, such bewilderment, and at last with such a patient and selfless love, is his own true voice? If the Archangel is to be served, there must be self-abnegation of this kind.

And though it is never explicitly stated, this question is near to the heart of all Shakespeare's work. Stated rather more fully, it is the question: how can a man bear authority within a community, and serve its true spirit, when he is a fallen being, not fully master of himself? It is easier for a poet to serve an Archangel than for a king; and yet what is a king, if the spirit of his country cannot speak through him? In almost every one of Shakespeare's plays this theme appears in some form though most evidently in the histories and tragedies. The first essential for a ruler is genuine self-knowledge — which he will not find if he turns his back upon real life, in search of wisdom, as the King of Navarre attempts to do in *Love's Labour's Lost*. When the king lies, he will infect the whole country as happens with Denmark in *Hamlet* and with Scotland in *Macbeth*. But how can he conceivably develop all the 'king-becoming graces' described by Malcolm in *Macbeth*?

> . . . justice, verity, temperance, stableness,
> Bounty, perseverance, mercy, lowliness,
> Devotion, patience, courage, fortitude . . .[9]

To possess all these would be to achieve something like perfect manhood; but men are not perfect. How can personal weaknesses like anger or jealousy be prevented from darkening the judgment of a king in the exercise of his authority? Lear and Leontes fail just in this way, and terrible consequences follow.

In quite a different realm of poetry, this theme had already been developed before the time of Shakespeare. In such early versions of the Grail story as those by Chrétien de Troyes and Wolfram von Eschenbach there is great stress on the figure of Amfortas, the King of the Grail whose wound cannot be healed. He can only lean, he cannot ride nor walk nor lie nor stand and at times the pain which he must suffer distresses all those around him. The whole Kingdom of the Grail falls into need. But the effects reach far beyond this Kingdom, and to the one who heals Amfortas a mysterious

39

power will be granted. When Sigune thinks that Parsifal has already accomplished this — though he has failed — she says 'You shall reign over all things, whatsoever the air touches, all creatures, tame and wild, shall serve you . . .'[10]

More and more as he approached the end of his work as a dramatist, Shakespeare brought in young figures able to heal the sickness of the King. In *All's Well that Ends Well* Helena heals quite simply by using the remedy inherited from her father, a physician who has died before the play begins. But the seriousness of her undertaking is shown by her willingness to die if her treatment fails. The sickness of Cymbeline is not evident physically, but in his inability to see the evil in his Queen. She is described as torturing animals with her experiments on poisons, and is warned by a genuine physician that no good will come of this. Shakespeare describes in this play in wonderful images the recovery of the influence of the true Archangel. Imogen, daughter of Cymbeline's first queen who has died, has to put on the disguise of a man, and journey to the far West of Britain. She finds her lost brothers, and when in their company seems to die, and is mourned by the incomparable song:

> Fear no more the heat o' th' sun
>   Nor the furious winter's rages;
> Thou thy worldly task hast done,
>   Home art gone, and ta'en thy wages.
> Golden lads and girls all must,
> As chimney-sweepers, come to dust.[11]

The words speak of death and dust, but in their music there is infinite promise. Whatever sickness has been endured in the body, whatever social injustice suffered, the soul will find in the realm of the Archangels after death renewed health and courage. And from the worlds of the dead help can come to the living. Imogen is able to find and rescue her lost husband Posthumus, for whom his dead parents and brothers have pleaded before the throne of eternal Justice.

When she goes to the West, Imogen is seeking the sources of enduring life for her country, as Gilgamesh did after the death of his friend. And so the wonderful final scene of reconciliation is achieved, in which everyone shares except the Queen. She has chosen her own dark way, the misuse of the powers of Nature.

To find the Archangel anew, there has always to be a recovery of understanding for the past. Most of Shakespeare's early plays are concerned with the kings of England; the young William Blake draws the figures on the tombs, all alone in Westminster Abbey. But this is not only a task for great artists; everyone is called to the understanding of his country's history, and to feel something of the atmosphere of places where great events happened. Nor is anyone concerned only with the Archangel of his own country; in sleep we seek the great shining Ring of spirits who inspire the nations of the earth. Nor is it only those who have the responsibilities of power who suffer the sickness of Amfortas. Almost everyone belongs to a community or communities, for which they share responsibility. Every teacher, or doctor or priest (to take a few examples) has a task which goes beyond his capacities; his limited human nature is in conflict with what is asked of him. Personal jealousies and private wishes strike at the roots of his vocation. He is entangled with problems for which there seem to be no solutions. For this reason very many people today can identify themselves, more or less consciously, with Hamlet or Shakespeare's other troubled heroes. Inwardly we are to become kings, sources of real community; we cannot accomplish this by our own powers, but only by accepting something that is given to us from the spiritual world.

Shakespeare often compares a king to the sun. But plainly no-one should make this sort of comparison about *himself*. It is the tragic misfortune of Richard II that he has not learned the distinction between the qualities of his own soul and the graces of kingliness which should work through him. He cannot hear the spirit of his country when it speaks through another voice, that of the dying John of Gaunt. The Archangels really have sun-like qualities; for their cosmic childhood was spent in Old Sun, a universe abounding in light and goodness, with a mood like the fragrance of a rose.

One of the Archangels has above all the qualities of the spiritual Sun. In the Bible he bears the name Michael. It is only from among the Archangels that the Bible tells us the names of particular spirits of the hierarchies. Once men knew many divine names, and felt it as a heavenly privilege to be able to speak them. But nearly all of them have been forgotten; and our progress in learning fitting names will be very slow. (Characteristically, in Plato's dialogue, *Cratylus*, Socrates begins his study of language with the names of the gods.) One interpretation of the name of Michael is 'Who is like God?'. Michael would have man hold in his heart the consciousness that he is like God, and is a little world reflecting the whole universe fashioned by God.

The leadership of a people is only one of the tasks fulfilled by the Archangels. There are some of them, headed by Michael, who inspire from time to time wide movements in civilization, lasting over several centuries. Rudolf Steiner mentioned in particular seven Archangels, who are leaders of such periods in succession. (This was known, and written about by learned men up to the beginning of the sixteenth century.) When a time of Michael comes, the challenge to feel the common humanity which is beyond all distinctions of nation or class is brought most strongly before the world. Since 1879 we have been living in such a time.

In the far past, human beings felt their moods of feeling and their impulses to action as belonging to earthly existence, but the real comprehension of the world as a communion with the Divine. A man could only be called wise when he was regarded as sharing the thoughts of God which lie behind earthly beings and events. By reaching towards the divine thoughts which lie behind historic conflicts, peace could be found. In the course of the ages, knowledge has come to seem more and more an earthly thing, achieved by our intelligence for our own uses. But the medieval Realist philosophers still preserved the conviction that universals — general concepts like 'man' or 'tree' — existed first in the mind of God, then dwell in the thing itself, and come finally to illumine the mind of man. Only when thoughts are really felt as capable of shining, as star-like in the mind, can this great conception awaken to full life within us.

Michael accepts it as cosmic fact that man has taken possession of his own intelligence; but would have him exercise it with a sense of profound responsibility towards the universe and towards the heavenly powers. Michael looks up to the Godhead, to the Divine Trinity with burning devotion; for him thinking and seeing are one. He seeks to found a great community among those men who can enliven their thinking so that it becomes transparent, a living in light, a breathing in light. This community can then be felt as enduring into the future, as working steadily for the redemption of the earth.

In the New Testament there are two passages where Michael is mentioned by name. One is in the Letter of Jude:

> But when the archangel Michael, contending with the devil, disputed about the body of Moses, he did not presume to pronounce a reviling judgment upon him, but said, 'The Lord rebuke you.'[12]

Michael will not speak to any being, or about any being, with scornful hostility, though he bears a sword. To wound or slander with words — in the sense of what is to be overcome on the Eightfold Path — are things quite alien to him. He can contend with Satan because he uses powers which come from the highest hierarchies. What is meant by the 'body of Moses'? There is a similar expression in the Revelation to John, where the bodies of the two witnesses,

Moses and Elijah, are described as lying in the street of the great city 'spiritually called Sodom and Egypt'[13], until they are raised by the power of God. A great spirit leaves behind him what is sometimes called a body of work. If this is not brought to life in the hearts of his successors, it is either treated as dogma or regarded with contempt; the tragic comparison with a corpse becomes possible. The Law which came through Moses can indeed live on in human hearts and unite men in a strong community; but it can also turn to stone in human minds and be hurled in condemnation against others or prove in one's own soul a deathly burden. Michael would have the Law grow into Love, as it does in the heart of Paul.

In the twelfth chapter of the Revelation to John we find the great heavenly Sign: the Woman clothed with the Sun, with a crown of twelve stars and with the moon under her feet. She is in the pains of birth, and is threatened by the dragon, who intends to devour her child. There follows the description of Michael's battle:

Now war arose in heaven, Michael and his angels fighting against the dragon; and the dragon and his angels fought, but they were defeated and there was no longer any place for them in heaven. And the great dragon was thrown down, that ancient serpent, who is called the Devil and Satan, the deceiver of the whole world—he was thrown down to the earth, and his angels were thrown down with him. And I heard a loud voice in heaven, saying, 'Now the salvation and the power and the kingdom of our God and the authority of his Christ have come, for the accuser of our brethren has been thrown down, who accuses them day and night before our God. And they have conquered him by the blood of the Lamb and by the word of their testimony, for they loved not their lives even unto death. Rejoice then, O heaven and you that dwell therein! But woe to you, O earth and sea, for the devil has come down to you in great wrath, because he knows that his time is short!'[14]

Many levels of existence, and many periods of history, can be illumined through the great apocalyptic Signs of the Woman clothed with the sun and of the battle of Michael with the Dragon. In this context we can think of them as picturing the birth in the soul of that greater Self which can lead man again into the companionship of the hierarchies. The soul from which the powers of the sun stream out in confidence and courage, with thoughts that shine like a great circle of stars; and, able to master the instinctive moon forces which work from the depths, brings to birth that true innermost self which is free from every taint of pride or self-seeking. Michael is the protector of this birth.

Before this freedom can be born, we have first to enter an earthly body. Our physical birth has another protector, the Archangel Gabriel. While Michael is described in the Bible in visions of the spirit, Gabriel appears in connection with physical places and times. Luke's Gospel describes the annunciation of John the Baptist to Zechariah in the temple at Jerusalem and the annunciation of Jesus to Mary in Nazareth. Gabriel proclaims these two moments, separated by about half a year. The souls who receive his tidings will be able to prepare for the great events which are coming. But Gabriel seeks to extend his wings over all mothers, and over fathers in so far as they are prepared to approach with reverence the mystery of birth and the souls who are to become their children. In the previous chapter the attempt was made to describe the entry of a soul into earthly existence as something which concerns the Angels. Among the Archangels, Gabriel is particularly close to what the Angels do, especially in the realm of birth and early childhood.

In our age it is more difficult than ever before to be a mother. What once seemed to come so naturally is now often wrapped in uncertainty and bewilderment. Parents turn anxiously to books about the care of babies — until even the writers of such books have to assure parents that they will do quite well without them. This is not to reject the possibility of mutual help among mothers — though all advice in this field should be given in a very undogmatic way. Babies are individuals, and do not all want the same things.

Gabriel inspires mothers with loving understanding for their own children. This often helps mothers to give children names which will guide and encourage them all their lives.

Gabriel works rather through feelings than in the realm of thoughts. Both father and mother may feel a great deal that guides them in providing a right environment for their children. Through the first months and years, the child will receive impressions that form him through his senses; from the walls and furniture of his room, from what grows in the garden, from people he meets, from places to which he is brought. His first vision of the sea may live with him always. But we may not receive the inspirations of Gabriel easily. What separates us from him most of all is lack of gratitude. Where there are young children, the whole atmosphere should be filled with thankfulness — for the existence of the children themselves, for food, for colours and tastes and sounds and smells, for sunlight and animals and all the world.

As children grow, another Archangel comes to have great significance for them, though this is hardly at all recognized in our time. Even the part of the Bible that deals with him has often been put into the Apocrypha or left out altogether; and few people seem to read it. But many artists have loved it, Rembrandt in particular; it is the Book of Tobit. Here we have something which perhaps lies between the spiritual realm in which Michael has been perceived and the course of earthly history into which Gabriel bears his promise; a parable set in earthly surroundings but with something of the quality of a fairy-tale.

During the Assyrian captivity the pious old Israelite, Tobit, does many good works. He buries with honour the bodies of any of his people he finds lying in the streets of Nineveh. His actions are an offence in the sight of the authorities. After one such deed, he lies in the courtyard of his house and the droppings of sparrows fall into his eyes and eventually blind him. He is reduced to poverty and misery, and is even reviled by his faithful wife Anna. He remembers that he once deposited a sum of money with a kinsman who lives in Media. Tobit's son Tobias is willing to make the journey to fetch it, and finds a companion to go with him.

At the time when Tobit is praying in despair the daughter of another kinsman of Tobit's, Raguel, also living in Media, is praying too in desperate need. Sarah has been married seven times, and each time her husband, before the consummation of his marriage to her, has been killed by a demonic power.

From the throne of God the Archangel Raphael is sent to help both Tobit and Sarah. It is he who accompanies Tobias and instructs him in all that he has to do, only revealing himself as an Archangel when he has brought Tobias with Sarah as his bride back to his father. Tobit, healed of his blindness, falls on his knees in praise and wonder as Raphael returns to God.

The story is told with a surprising gentleness and humour; to read it, hear it told, even to see scenes from it acted or painted, is to open oneself to a healing influence.

In the Book of Tobit, Raphael declares himself as 'one of the seven holy angels who present the prayers of the saints and enter into the presence of the glory of the Holy One'[15]. The old tradition, confirmed by Rudolf Steiner, which assigns the Archangels to Sun, Moon, and the five visible planets known to antiquity, assigns Raphael to Mercury. We may picture him with the winged staff of Mercury, around which two serpents ascend in spirals, one dark and one light. For the understanding of the work of Raphael, this symbol has far-reaching significance. He is the interpreter of one world to another, the mediator between what is above and what is below, between light and dark, between conscious and the unconscious. Michael calls for the greatest wakefulness; Gabriel is deeply concerned with the part of man that sleeps, even in the day. It is the work of Raphael to bring about a harmonious interplay between day and night. We can be healed, because we both wake and sleep. Illness comes about when we are withered by too much consciousness or flooded by unconscious powers.

All those who truly work for healing are members of the community of Raphael. It is indeed always a matter of community; one man alone could never heal. Everyone who works in this realm needs the support and understanding of others whether from among the living or from among the dead. It is never one person's cleverness alone which can bring health; the kind of intelligence that is needed comes about when earthly thoughts are lifted up, like the serpents on Mercury's staff, towards the grace coming from above. Thus Raphael works very closely with Michael.

In the names of the days of the week, we have the remnant of an ancient wisdom concerning the planets. If we take the Latin names, the sequence is quite plain: Saturn's day, Sun's day, Moon's day, Mars's day, Mercury's day, Jupiter's day, Venus's day. In modern languages various changes have been made, but the underlying sequence is the same. This sequence has not, and has never had, an obvious, immediate relation to the positions and rhythms of the visible planets and heavenly bodies of our present universe. It is related to the great sequence of universes to which reference has been made.

The sequence of the Archangels is the same as the sequence of the weekdays — only in the opposite direction through time. In the week Monday, the Moon's day, follows Sunday. In the course of the centuries, the period of the Moon-Archangel Gabriel precedes that of the Sun-Archangel Michael; and so through the whole sequence. Thus before the age of Gabriel, which began in the sixteenth century, there was the period of the Mars-Archangel, Samael, a time of many tragic conflicts — but also of the awakening of much spiritual courage. (Shakespeare's histories, from *King John* to *Henry VIII*, span almost exactly the 320 years of Samael's period.) Before the Mars period there was the Mercury period of Raphael; the earlier Middle Ages, from the ninth to the twelfth centuries. It was at the end of this period that the Grail story became known in Europe.

Raphael had to prepare beforehand for times of great danger to mankind. Civilization would before long be governed by an entirely earthly intelligence. The age of the machine was approaching. At the same time it was becoming more and more difficult for men to prevent those passions, which had long wrought havoc in human communities, from invading the part of man dedicated to the spiritual world as well. The story of the Grail was both a warning and a promise. As we have seen, it warned all those in positions of leadership and responsibility how great and difficult the task of self-knowledge is; but it promised the awakening of capacities in man which would enable him to carry responsibility in humility and innocence, as Parsifal does.

The revelation which enables Parsifal to become King of the Grail is given to him on Good Friday. It is with the kind of freshness of a spring landscape around him that he hears the earnest words of Trevrizent. He learns the significance of his own failures and can relate them to the Mystery of Golgotha. He has received the diagnosis of a wise physician and knows the remedy. It is a revelation from Raphael. And it is in the spring, during the present age too, that we can open ourselves best of all to the inspirations of Raphael, teaching us about the nature of our sickness and the healing power of the Resurrection. We can celebrate the Christmas festival in the gentle light of Gabriel, in so far as it is a festival for children and for the child in all men. Going back in thought to autumn we find the great challenge of the Michaelmas festival summoning man to battle with the dragon-nature of sloth and anxiety within him. The Parsifal in each man wakens to the whole life of the year.

There is yet another mysterious being, of whom both the Bible, and the spiritual research of Rudolf Steiner, have something to say, though very little. In the abundant stillness of midsummer, from the day of John the Baptist onwards, a quality is to be felt which is unlike all the other moods of nature, a deep questioning. It is as if man were being reminded that he does not belong only to the world he knows, but to something quite different as well, something beyond all the past and future he can imagine. Time is in debt to eternity. There is a great spirit who tells man of all the worlds in which he has a share, which he must serve in their turn; a spirit who speaks in man's deepest conscience. This spirit is named Uriel.

Always the Archangels call men together, to find each other in greater ways than in the ordinary concerns of life. Seeking their realm, we are aided by a mighty wind, which blows across the world.

3. The Archai

From birth to death, during our waking hours, we live in the world of the senses, and this impresses us as reality. This world is richer and more varied in character than we generally notice. There are certain senses which particularly impress man as he is today with a feeling of inescapable reality. When he touches a hard object, or tries to move something which he feels as heavy, these experiences seem to guarantee that he is encountering a reality. But if he hears a word spoken, he may be inclined to feel that this is in some way less real than a stone or a piece of wood.

It is possible to differentiate the senses in a way that forms a kind of scale, conveying to us varying qualities of reality. Through touch, we seem to be meeting outer objects in the most definite way, outside the limits of our body. But we also experience in a very powerful way conditions within the body itself — comfort and discomfort, vitality and weariness, for example. The sense that conveys to us the presence of these conditions can be called the sense of life. Then we have a sense of how our own body is related to weight and lightness, the sense of balance, and closely connected with it the sense of our own movements. With these four realms we have to do from very early childhood through our efforts of will. We come then to senses to which we respond very strongly through our feelings: the senses of warmth, smell, taste and sight. Warmth, smell, and taste are still linked very closely with our awareness of conditions in our own body. But with sight we seem to be achieving a greater objectivity; our likes and dislikes do not press on us quite so urgently. And we see many things we cannot touch; the blue sky, the stars, the rainbow, shadows and much else.

Sight is concerned with a threefold encounter; between

light, the surfaces of things, and ourselves. When we hear, we are concerned with a meeting of qualities that lie beneath the surfaces of things; when we hear the wind in trees, for example, we are participating in the meeting between the inner nature of air and the inner nature of branches. Sound opens the way to the experience of other sentient beings; we begin to share in the pain of an animal which cries out, or in the triumph and happiness of birds. And when we listen to other human beings, other, subtler senses come to our aid; the sense for the sounds of speech, and the sense for the thoughts which speech can express. (In English we have the admirable phrase 'I see what you mean' — and in other languages there are comparable expressions showing that we feel the meeting with another's thought as something which can be compared to sight, or taste, or even smell.) Finally, when we meet another person, not necessarily in conversation, but perhaps only in seeing each other, the sense for the other's individuality is stirred; we use what may be called the most delicate of human senses, the I-sense — which need not convey to us anything that is self-assertive in the other, but simply the presence of another being capable of perception and thought.

Through birth and early childhood we plunged into this abundant, manifold ocean of perception; in sleep and death we are drawn away from it into another kind of reality. And it is easy to suppose that men in their waking hours on earth have always had exactly the same experience of the senses that we have now. Some descriptions of reincarnation appear to confirm this; as if each life brought the same delights and pains, the same forms and colours, the same illuminating or puzzling experience of what others say. But an attentive reading of what was written even a few centuries ago can show that the matter is not so simple. When we come again, we do not really see the same world. Contours have become more definite, processes more calculable. We are much less aware of the presence of the divine in things, than we were in incarnations long ago. Even today, there are subtle differences in the consciousness of human beings native to different parts of the earth. And yet in general what has been said about the powerful reality conveyed by the sense of touch, and the response of feeling to what may be called the middle senses, is valid at the present time. We are men of our age; and once we were men of other ages, with quite different feelings about the borderline between the spiritual and the physical.

Just as there are spiritual beings, the Archangels, who are concerned with leading souls into the right national community for them, and with inspiring the history of that nation, so there are spiritual beings who lead human souls into successive civilizations, and who so shape those civilizations that they will provide the right experiences for those who incarnate within them. These spirits are called in Greek *Archai*, a word which can be rendered Princes, or Principalities; the basic sense is that they are the first among many, bearers of the purposes which lived at the beginnings of things. Rudolf Steiner spoke of them as Spirits of Personality. They form successive civilizations in such a way that man develops towards personality on earth, feeling himself in ancient times only as part of a tribal community, passing through stages in which he has a status given to him from outside, towards the awakening of a freedom in which he chooses the purposes and tasks of his life for himself.

The Archai live in glowing enthusiasm for the awakening of man into free understanding and free action. As the Angels are akin to patiently flowing water, and the Archangels to the swift-moving winds of heaven, the Archai are fiery spirits, enkindling and purifying love. And just as the Archangels wish to have the nations entrusted to them live as part of a great choir, each contributing voices in accord with the rest, so would the Archai have every age bring its part in the whole development of man, from the first beginnings to the fulfilment of history, from Alpha to Omega.

An age grows cold for the Archai when it sinks into sterile

repetition and routine. They will that man should look at the works of his age, and of previous ages, with an enthusiasm like their own. And they help men and women to share in the most varied ways in the creative work of each civilization. In general a soul needs at least one incarnation as a man, and one incarnation as a woman, in each age of mankind. In the past masculine incarnations have often been strongly coloured by action, feminine incarnations by suffering. But the positive creative work which could be done by men and by women has often been different; and through these varieties of work they have been able to refine the experience of the senses in different ways. In the far past each kind of work, even the most ordinary, was felt indeed as the service of a special god or goddess, who had to be suitably invoked before the work began. The things of earth could only be rightly touched and transformed in a mood of reverence and prayer.

The Angels are concerned, as we have tried to see, with our sensitivity in thinking, and our near personal relationships. The Archangels breathe in and seek to influence the character of human speech, leading the development of language so that it may become a true bridge between human souls. The Archai are deeply attentive to what a human being does, particularly when his work has a significance for wider circles of people and for the life of Nature. And in the end almost everything we do has such significance. When we sleep, the Archai observe whether our deeds were good for the world in which we live during the day. When men felt their work as a consecrated service of divine beings, it was acceptable for the realm of the Archai. For modern man, it is quite difficult to imagine that ordinary work should have anything to do with spiritual beings. And if the name of God is invoked in connection with everyday things, this is often done without the necessary reverence and depth. But not long ago men could call upon the Godhead and upon spiritual beings for help in the details of earthly work in ways that are not at all incongruous or trivial. Wonderful examples can again be found in Alexander Carmichael's collection of verses from the Gaelic. There are many instances from the work of the shepherd.

> The Three who are above in the city of glory,
> Be shepherding my flock and my kine,
> Tending them duly in heat, in storm, and in cold,
> With the blessing of power driving them down
> From yonder height to the sheiling fold.

> The name of Ariel of beauteous bloom,
> The name of Gabriel herald of the Lamb,
> The name of Raphael prince of power,
> Surrounding them and saving them.[16]

In some parts of the Western Isles the work of the weaver was done mainly by women, in others by men. But the loom itself was felt as a feminine being. There was a prayer for the session of work of Saturday, looking towards the next week:

> In name of Mary, mild of deeds,
> In name of Columba, just and potent,
> Consecrate the four posts of my loom,
> Till I begin on Monday.

> Her pedals, her sleay, and her shuttle,
> Her reeds, her warp and her cogs,
> Her cloth-beam and her thread-beam,
> Thrums and the thread of the plies.

> Every web, black, white, and fair,
> Roan, dun, checked, and red,
> Give thy blessing everywhere,
> On every shuttle passing under the thread.

> Thus will my loom be unharmed
> Till I shall arise on Monday;
> Beauteous Mary will give me of her love,
> And there shall be no obstruction I shall not overcome.[17]

In such verses, whether in Christian tradition or reaching back to the earliest cultures of which we have any record, there is often an explicit comparison between the work of men and the work of heavenly spirits; and perhaps this comparison is always there in the underlying mood of the words. The heavenly powers are shepherds, guarding men from danger; and they are the weavers of human fate. Vishvakarman is the world-carpenter, Hephaestos the god who works as a smith. In ancient Rome, man has to put aside the weapons of Mars at the door which is guarded by Janus and approach with a humble and gentle heart the hearth which is blessed by Vesta.

We can see that it was natural for men to have such feelings when so many of the things which they did were closer to great archetypal activities, which they could regard as having been taught to their ancestors by gods or heroes near to the gods. Human beings saw in each other whether work was good, and done with love. The work acceptable in the community would also be acceptable to the spiritual beings to whom its significance would be carried by souls during sleep. But there was one of the gods who was concerned with many changes in the character of human work. In Latin he is called Mercury. The spiritual beings behind this name had indeed to do with one of the holiest and most ancient of human activities, the work of the healer. But in quite early times human beings were willing to travel to strange places in search of a healer, and healers were themselves willing to travel, in search both of deeper knowledge of their art and of people who needed their help. And other servants of the Mercury-power also learned to travel far, making themselves acceptable in strange communities because they brought rare and precious things, some of them indeed for use in healing. The work of the merchant begins, and still has its divine exemplar; the very words *merchant* and *commerce* are related linguistically to the name Mercury. But it seems that in the earliest Indo-European language, before it was diversified into its great branches, there was no name for this occupation or the person who followed it.

What the merchant brought was the result of somebody's work. The precious metals and jewels had been found or mined, the furs brought in by the hunter. But the man who obtained the wares from the merchant could no longer see the man who had first worked upon them. The merchant might indeed deceive him about them. The origin of money is closely connected with the work of the merchant and with the possibility of deceit. Here too the blessing of heaven is at first invoked. Many of the earliest coins bear the image of the goddess of the city, a kind of heavenly guarantee of the quality and amount of the metal they contain. When men first began to put *their* image and superscription upon coins, it was something near to blasphemy, a rash comparison of the mortal with the immortal. And as purchase supersedes barter, heavenly and earthly judgments on the works of men go asunder. What was once a visible market-place, where seller and buyer meet face to face, grows wider and wider, until in our time it covers the whole earth. With the extent of the market the degree of specialization increases. The machine can enter work more and more; and men carry into sleep the effects of work which they may be less and less able to understand, and about which they themselves may be deceived.

In our time there is a widespread longing to return to kinds of work nearer to the heavenly archetypes. Farming, fishing, weaving, work with wood — such occupations begin to be followed for their own sake. And yet there is an uneasy sense that it is not possible to everyone to make this kind of choice. The development from the village to world economy was not just a mistake. Have not the Archai themselves led us upon this way? The change in the character of human work does indeed contribute to the growth of human freedom. Ancient economic communities held men and women to the status and the task to which they were born. Today there is a vast and often bewildering opportunity for choice in many countries of the world. We saw it is sometimes possible within a single life to make several changes of occupation, not necessarily dictated by outer circumstances, but springing perhaps from quiet inner consideration of the needs of others. Work which is done for people we do not see may not be at all a cold and impersonal thing, if we have some feeling for humanity in general. And this is the crux of the matter. An engine-driver, for example, may have a deep sense of responsibility for the people travelling behind him, even if he has not seen any of them — though it might have been good if he had. Increasingly it is becoming possible for everyone to form some picture of the joys and sufferings, the hopes and needs, of people in widely varying circumstances far way from us in space. It is often thought that love for humanity as a whole must be a very thin kind of love; and yet evidence can be found that this is by no means always true.

With every conceivable kind of work, it is possible for those engaged in it to grow in understanding for its significance for the world. Warmth can flow into this understanding; the warmth of a selfless willingness to serve the needs of other people, however diverse in outlook and character they may be. Work done in this way can be in full accord with the aims of the Archai, however uninteresting it may appear. But there is very much in our present economic order which hinders the development of this relationship to work. It can be marred by many kinds of group selfishness; aggressive nationalism, and the desire for power and profit by those belonging to some trade or profession, can have a poisonous influence upon what is done.

In the New Testament an *archon* is spoken of, who is the opponent of the work of the Archai. He is described as 'the ruler of this world'[18] and has nothing to do with the Spirit of Christ. Under his influence, people can regard all sorts of distortion in the economic order, brought about by arbitrary power or the desire for power, as natural and acceptable. He tries to tear away the present age from all other ages, whether as these were in the past, or as they should be in the future according to the purposes of those spirits from whom man has his origin. The stamp of the prince of this world is more evident on many things which meet our senses at present, especially in cities, than the signature of the true Archai. Even when we visit some great achievement of another age, for example Stonehenge|or another monument of the kind, it may be very difficult to attain tranquillity or the active imagination which are needed if we are to feel its purpose.

By our work we do not only influence each other, and the spirits above us. Whatever we do has its effects on the whole earth. Only in this century has anything like the universal recognition of this come about, under the impact of inescapable events — though much earlier ages were aware of it in a different way. We know something about the poisoning of birds, the destruction of wild species, the pollution of the seas and of the atmosphere. We have begun to doubt the rightness of taking human desires as the decisive test for what should happen on the earth. But even if we start to take into account the right of the animals, of growing things, even of seas and mountains to exist in their own way, we are still leaving out half the inhabitants of Earth. Other ages saw, we do not see, the hosts of elemental beings around us. The Archai have led us into a certain clarity of sense perception, through which we are aware in the world around us, of what can be measured, counted, and weighed. We have indeed gone beyond the intentions of the Archai, letting the senses over-impress us with the reality and solidity of what they reveal; we have allowed them to stupefy us, more than a little. Now the Archai seek to awaken us to the more delicate qualities of all that reaches us through the senses; particularly to the subtle contrasts of colour and colour, of tone and tone. We can observe that what comes to us through the senses very much depends on what we are seeking. If we look for objects, they will tell us about objects. If we regard movement as a series of positions, they will tell us about positions. If we think of all shadows as grey or black, we shall see them so. From a world of great abundance and delicacy, we choose out what we believe we need, and are in danger of disregarding all but the crudest aspects of our environment.

But we are surrounded by beings who would like us to attend to our senses with much more reverence, so that our experience would be nearer to theirs. For them objects in themselves are of very little interest. They are deeply concerned with relationships; with the meetings and partings of beings and substances. How a root finds its way through the soil, how a leaf moves in the wind, how smoke comes out of a chimney, how an aroma enters a nose — such things have great significance for them. They do not possess things, as we claim to do. Change is their natural element, rigidity a strange effort. Not only in his senses, but in his whole being they would like man to be far more active. Man helps to liberate them from their burdens when he makes efforts to understand the world, when he is industrious, when he is happy, and when he is filled with awe and wonder. Stupidity, carelessness, and morose or moody feelings can distress them greatly. And today we bring the elementals new problems as well. Just as some creatures and plants need hedges, many of the elementals need the varied borders and encounters provided by nature, which man used to find natural as well. Monoculture can be terrible for the elementals. Even a plant very pleasant in itself can be dreadful if grown by the million. A field that is the right size and shape for machine harvesting may be the wrong size and shape for the elementals who keep the crops healthy. It may be a long time before such things show in agricultural statistics; people notice first the decline in aroma or flavour, but eventually in quantities as well.

It is not only through the invasion of agriculture by technology that we make new problems for the elemental beings. Everything that we do enters their realm in one way or another. Our sense of touch, for example, is often trying to tell us whether a substance is being used with the right feeling for its character or not, for it is only in our heads that we are really isolated from the life of the elementals; otherwise we are immersed in it. When we respond to any kind of beauty, for example, we are very close to them — except that beauty or lack of beauty may be for them a much more urgent matter than it may seem to us.

There is great diversity among the elementals, as in the rest of nature. There are kinds which play a particularly helpful part in the general order of things, and others which are more destructive or self-absorbed. Tradition tells us of four categories which are very helpful to plants and animals and stand near to the purposes of the hierarchies in general. Their traditional names are gnomes, undines, sylphs and salamanders. The gnomes move unhindered through rock and ore, and care for the root development in plants. The undines live in flowing water and rising sap, helping the plant on its way to air and light. The sylphs fly with the winds, and touch leaf and petal with their gracious power. The salamanders or fire spirits work in the ripening of fruit and seed, gleaming with deep content in the summer and autumn air. Though the elementals are lesser beings than the spirits of the hierarchies, they have all a close kinship with the Angels, Archangels and Archai. Rudolf Steiner calls these elementals 'offspring' of the spirits of the hierarchies; the gnomes of the Archai, the undines of the Archangels, the sylphs of the Angels. The fire spirits seem to have a more complex and mysterious origin.

In the human realm the relationship between offspring and parent sometimes appears a little puzzling. And it may seem hard to connect in thought the fiery creative love of the Archai with the glittering intelligence of the gnomes which sometimes appears scornful, though they *can* show this quality when contemplating man. Towards the earth as a whole the gnomes are filled with limitless patience and devotion. Like the Archai from whom they come they are concerned with the solidification of the earth, and its eventual disintegration. The earth will die, just as each human being has to die. What matters is how we and the earth grow towards death. Man's irresponsibility threatens to shatter the earth prematurely, before its full purposes are achieved.

The concern of the gnomes for the life and death of the earth can be compared with the case of the Archai for successive civilizations. Each of these shapes many material things — temples, cities, works of art, and tools. Far the greater part of these are destroyed and leave little trace. If this did not happen, there would not be room for another civilization to come. The true Archai accept this, and see that what is essential in every achievement passes over into the spiritual world and lives on. But there are many misleading spirits who tempt man with an illusion of permanence — both for things he makes, and above all for institutions. Or they inspire the conception that a civilization will go on and on developing in precisely the same direction; that our present world, for instance, will go on and on producing more and more complex machines, without any real change happening in our minds and hearts.

Man comes to the aid of the elementals when he does something which outwardly appears simple, but which embodies great and warm ideas. At the heart of every civilization there have been such ritual acts. A religious faith endures and grows not primarily because of its teachings but because such things are done and deeply felt within it. It is not possible to fulfil such ritual acts with their full significance if material things are regarded without any reverence, as material things and nothing more. When water is used in Christian baptism for example, we need some feeling for the mystery of water, some ideas about the part it plays in the universe, not limited to those of ordinary chemistry and physics. Something has been contributed towards this in recent years when we have looked towards bodies in the solar system bereft of water, and felt in contrast the blessedness of our misty earth. When a baptism is fulfilled with a consciousness of how water serves the whole mystery of birth, in the way the form of baptism celebrated in

The Christian Community leads us to do, our feeling for water in all its everyday uses can begin to change too. All the sacraments, as they have been reborn in this century in The Christian Community, contribute to that deepening of our life in the senses which is needed in our time; all of the twelve senses mentioned at the beginning of this chapter are included in this. What has existed before in us on very different levels, often in conflict with one another — our judgments of good and evil, our sense of beauty and ugliness, our likes and dislikes — comes to be related within us in a much more harmonious, light-filled way.

It was necessary that humanity should find itself within a world that seems empty of moral quality, regulated only by some mathematical principle, or perhaps only by chance. In this universe man has to seek in his own deepest being for a purpose for his existence. Through the presence of the small seed of love within him his perceptions and ideas begin to change. He meets once more living and perceptive spirits of kinds other than his own, who have also purposes; and his can grow into harmony with theirs. The physical work which had seemed to have so limited a significance begins to promise effects that will endure when all material things have vanished away. When there is no selfless love in what we do there are no lasting consequences; what is done in genuine response to human needs, will go on. In St Luke's Gospel the story of the Good Samaritan is told as part of the answer to the question, 'What shall I do to inherit eternal life?' (The story need not be taken as 'just a parable'. There can well have been a particular physical Samaritan who did this, just as there is a physical site for the inn to which he came. But the story is also one of the greatest of all parables.)

The Archai seek the eternal within the temporal. This is part of their great preparation for the task which lies before them when our present universe has passed away. They will then rise to the rank of world creators and bring forth from the invisible, in accord with the purposes of still greater powers, a new heaven and a new earth.

The Second Hierarchy

4. Exousiai — the Spirits of Form

When we approach in thought the beings of the hierarchies, and try to ascend from the Archai to the beings called in Greek *Exousiai* we come to a great transition. For what is done by Angels, Archangels and Archai for man is primarily a work upon the human soul, and can be compared to the work of a human teacher or leader. But what is done by beings of the Second Hierarchy is very different from anything that can be done by man. They are creators; over great spaces they call life into being, and transform living things over long ages. Of all the processes that we encounter during life on earth, what we see as the effects of the sun upon living things are most comparable to what is brought about by their power. But our senses do not reach directly into the realm where they are manifest. We are aware of the light of the sun — though what we see is not the light itself, but the results of its encounter with surfaces, as has been described. The light and the darkness with which we are familiar extend a veil before us, hiding other lights and other forms of darkness much more rich in change and yet more enduring. Everything that lives and grows depends upon this realm, just beyond the reach of our senses. It opens up before the finer organs of perception which are now beginning to develop again in humanity; and we may be stirred to some awareness of it when we begin to pass from waking consciousness into sleep, or back again.

No traditional words are very satisfactory for the description of this realm. Rudolf Steiner used words which can be rendered in English 'etheric' or 'ethereal' or 'formative forces'. For the events of this realm a different kind of geometry and mathematics has to be applied, which does already exist, though it is comparatively little known.

Part of what happens in this realm has always been compared to our experience of sound: but it is not carried by vibrations in the air or other material substances. Thus in ancient creation stories we find descriptions of divine beings who speak, and the power of their words brings about mighty cosmic changes. The world as we know it is the result of these words spoken by divine beings. For example, in the Finnish epic, *Kalevala*, a wise old man tells Vainamoinen that the great flow of blood from his wound can be halted by true words of understanding:

> Stemmed before were greater torrents,
> Greater floods than this were hindered,
> By three words of the Creator,
> By the mighty words primeval.
> Brooks and streams were checked from flowing,
> Mighty streams in cataracts falling,
> Bays were formed in rocky headlands,
> Tongues of land were linked together.[19]

Both in the Old Testament and the New there are such descriptions. St John's Gospel speaks of the Word which was with God, and of how all things came into being through the Word. It should be remembered that the Greek *Logos* was much richer and wider in meaning than anything we can say today. It included order and proportion, significance and power. For those brought up under the influence of old Hebrew wisdom or early Greek philosophy, or of both, it was no difficult transition when St John goes on 'In him was life, and the life was the light of men'.

In Genesis, the first great deed of creation is generally translated 'And God said, "Let there be light"; and there was light'[20]. It should be remembered that here light is not yet differentiated into the lights of sun, moon and stars; all that follows is to be grounded in this light of the very beginning. Who is it, who brings this light into being through the power of the Word? It might seem quite unnecessary to ask this question: is it not the One God to whose worship all the Law and the Prophets bring witness? The word used here in Hebrew is Elohim; and much learned criticism of the Hebrew Bible has been concerned with the question of the use of the names 'Elohim' and 'Yahweh'. The word 'Elohim' is a plural and later on the text describes the Elohim as saying 'we' and 'our image'. Generally this is taken as a kind of royal plural, expressing the divine majesty. But the forms which language takes in ancient holy writings and in solemn pronouncements are to be considered seriously. We have tried to see how in ancient times a king did not regard himself just as a solitary individual but as the bearer of purposes brought to him from the spiritual world. In his pronouncements the Archangel of his country or other spiritual powers greater than himself, should be speaking with him. The 'we' was once felt as real, not just as formal. Later on in Genesis, at the annunciation of Isaac, there are wonderful transitions between the Godhead felt as One and as differentiated among several beings[21].

Modern man is inclined to seek a clear 'either–or'; something is said, for instance, either by God or by an Archangel. But for the old writings these are not mutually exclusive at all; something is said by God through an Archangel. A true Archangel does not speak, unless the divine will works through him. Thus it is not a rejection of the translation 'God' if it is said that Elohim is a real plural, and calls our attention to a particular rank of spiritual beings. Rudolf Steiner says that the original sense of the Hebrew 'Elohim' is the same as that of the Greek word 'Exousiai' as used in the work attributed to Dionysius the Areopagite. They are the spirits we are trying to approach, the lowest rank of the Second Hierarchy, whom Rudolf Steiner often calls 'Spirits of Form'. It is their work which is described in the Six Days of Creation in Genesis.

This work of creation is generally taken by those who study the Bible today in a much too external and material way. The Exousiai are not here to be thought of as creating separate material objects, but archetypal forms. It is one of the great confusions of modern thinking to imagine that the reality in far ancient times was what modern man would have seen and touched and understood, if he had been there. He was not there: no consciousness like his yet existed. It is quite unreal to suppose that a world looking like ours was then the real thing. It is quite hard for us to achieve this perception, and to keep it; the world as we perceive it today keeps slipping back into our minds. But what was real then was what one rank or other of beings perceived and understood then.

At the beginning of Genesis we are being raised into the consciousness of Exousiai, the Spirits of Form. Their living, shining thoughts are bringing into being the forms which will in time to come be embodied, though imperfectly, in particular earthly things. Having brought these forms into existence spiritually, not yet materially, they rejoice in their beauty and goodness. The forms express the purposes of many beings higher than the Exousiai themselves, and will shelter the experience of many beings less than them. The Six Days' design is, as it were, the great scene on which there can be many encounters, many ways of working together, many conflicts and tensions. They lead from the primeval light, through the differentiation of waters and of the solid earth, through the unfolding of the heavens, to the forms of sea creatures and birds, and to those of animals and man. And here there is something to which we should be attentive. In the second chapter of Genesis it is said that 'there was no man to till the ground'[22] — and then the formation of man of dust from the ground follows. What comes into being on the Sixth Day is not yet earthly man, but the spiritual archetype of the human being in heavenly thought. What Genesis brings is not two different creation stories patched together, but two events in the evolution of man, both of them immensely significant: and they happen at different levels of existence.

Underlying the text of the Sixth Day of Creation, though it

is not evident either in the Hebrew or in the translations we have, is the conception that in the original archetype of man masculine and feminine qualities were completely one. What the Exousiai bring into being is an image complete and perfect. They draw together into one form the forces that come from every direction of the universe; the microcosm as the full reflection of the macrocosm. This has as potentiality to fill the earth, and to rule over all living creatures. But the forms of man and woman, as these are present in the material world, only come about later, through the events described with great profundity in the second chapter of Genesis. Eve is there said to be made from the rib of Adam. This is the work of the power called, from the fourth verse of this chapter onwards. 'Yahweh-Elohim'. The description here bears witness to a life in the body which is beginning to draw near to the limitations of earth existence, though only after the Fall are they present with all their effect.

It has always been a difficult task for the human soul to approach with its own powers of comprehension and imagination the original archetype of humanity. A form which is neither man nor woman, nor with the marks of any race, invaded by no darkness or heaviness or weariness or pain — how can we picture this, or in any way represent it? The contemplation of this question can help us to understand why the people of Israel are later forbidden to make any image of the Godhead. Man is indeed this image: but who dare imagine or represent him in his perfect form? We have gone a long way from this great seriousness today, when no advertiser hesitates to use the image of earthly man to draw attention to the most trivial of his products.

In what way are the Exousiai concerned with the evolution of earthly man, into whom the archetypal form is to shine? It is evident that the name 'Yahweh' has to do with this evolution. Rudolf Steiner spoke many times of the profound significance of this name. It is used to designate one particular being belonging to the ranks of the Exousiai. The archetype of humanity is the work of seven Elohim, serving in unity the Godhead beyond all the hierarchies. Of these seven, Yahweh is one who takes on a specific task; to lead man into a close far-reaching relationship with the earth. The Fall is the work of Lucifer; it is met, not through a decision to take man away from the earth, but to make him so thoroughly an earthly being, united so strongly with earthly things, that at the last a fallen earth can be redeemed through him. This conception of Yahweh can help us with countless riddles of the Old Testament.

When the people of Israel sought Yahweh through the contemplation of their own destinies, they looked back at the mystery of birth. Each had been sent to his father and mother by Yahweh just as Isaac had been sent to Abraham and Sarah. His strength, and his weaknesses also were to be understood when he saw how his ancestors had obeyed or had disobeyed Yahweh. His own obedience brought the promise of blessings for those descended from him. Israel possessed a very deep sense of community and of individual responsibility as well. Their God said of himself 'I am the I am'[23]. Yahweh brings what may be called the first sense of individuality, through the experience of the separate earthly body, in its loneliness and its dignity.

Because we inhabit an earthly body, we do not only look back through time to birth, but forwards through time to death. And this is a great riddle for us, indeed the greatest of riddles. If the archetypal form were fully present within the human being, the body would not be vulnerable or sick; it would not be brought into the power of death. There is no death in the heavens — only life that is ever transformed, ever renewed. The earthly body hardens so far that it can no longer remain the instrument of the soul and spirit, which are unable to transform it.

The development of the human body on earth is not simple. It is the intention of the heavens that man should become a free being. His archetypal form has meaning as dwelling-place for this free being. And as the soul grows into individuality, out of the original dream-like sense of

71

community, the body becomes more ready to contain it. The Archai work steadily towards this goal. But the power of Lucifer is exerted to develop in the soul a premature sense of freedom. An eager desire for earthly experience grows up in the soul: and this extends to an attachment to earthly things through which freedom can be exercised. At the same time as the body is growing towards genuine freedom, it suffers harm from the intensity of the wishes springing up in the soul. It becomes both too earthly and too feverish. The diversity of the sexes has been brought about by the good powers: but Lucifer seeks to exploit it by making the soul one-sided, too much absorbed in earthly action during male incarnations, too much possessed by emotion during female incarnations. The true individuality constantly seeks to redress the balance.

Lucifer is followed by his shadow, Ahriman, the spirit of lies. And it can be foreseen by the good powers that Lucifer and Ahriman working together may be able to corrupt both the body and the soul of man so far, that the age-old heavenly intentions for man may be brought to nothing. There may never be a soul which can dwell truly in that body of which the Exousiai have prepared the archetypal form.

In many old representations of the crucifixion of Christ, the sun and the moon are shown above the cross. There is a profound significance in this. The moon represents the care and concern of Yahweh for man's fate on earth: the sun, the care and concern of the other six Elohim who had worked together for the creation of the earth. The earth is darkened; the primeval light is lost. But on the cross in the body of man there suffers that divine Being to whom the Elohim have once looked up in heights beyond the Seraphim, whose Word had sounded through them as they created.

The Christ lives in a vulnerable, suffering, and mortal body. But the strong powers of soul which grow up through his presence in Jesus promise the healing of every sickness. His soul is worthy of the archetypal form: when it is said of him, 'Behold the man!' this is true as it would not have been of any other. Of heavenly beings he alone experiences what human existence is. He alone experiences from within the meaning of human death.

The day of the crucifixion is Friday, which recalls the Sixth Day of Creation when the Elohim worked on the spirit-forms of the animals and of man. On the day when he should remember his own creation, man brings death to the being who gives the human form its true sense, who fills it truly. After the dead body has been laid in the tomb, there follows the day of stillness, the Sabbath. Then on the first day of the week, the day of primordial, not yet differentiated light, women and men begin to meet the Christ in his risen form.

Quite early in his work, the Christ had foretold his death and resurrection. According to the Gospel of St John, about the time of the first Passover described in the Gospel, Jesus had said 'Destroy this temple, and in three days I will raise it up'. And the evangelist says 'He spoke of the temple of his body'. It is not only at the time of the crucifixion that this temple is destroyed; through long ages men have desecrated the body entrusted to them as dwelling-place. They have used it as if it were of their own making, to do with it as they pleased. On Good Friday, long ages of misuse come to a head; the whole body is subjected to destructive violence. What the Christ builds anew is not the same body. It is not always even recognized as his at first. It can appear within a closed house, and vanish from sight. It can be seen and touched like a mortal body and yet is not mortal.

In Luke's Gospel, Jesus is described as saying: 'See my hands and my feet, that it is I myself; handle me, and see; for a spirit has not flesh and bones as you see that I have.'[24] What once the Elohim beheld in spirit, is now accomplished. When Jesus walked on earth between the Baptism in Jordan and Golgotha, the body was indeed filled with the soul and spirit worthy of it, but the body itself was one fallen from its archetypal being into the limitations of earth. For the eyes of the disciples it was not usually transparent, as it were, for the being within it. But now they had before them the Temple in its full splendour; no longer capable of injury at the hands of men. And what the disciples saw was not just the heavenly form beheld by the Elohim, in realms above the earth; the form now bore within it and manifested the experience of earthly life and death.

It has been a difficult task for the greatest artists to represent this. In scenes that follow the Resurrection, the Christ must appear as one who has overcome death, and has life and strength without limit; and yet the agony of death is behind him. The body is perfect; and yet it bears wounds. When Paul beholds the Christ in the fullness of primordial Light, he has no doubt at all that it is the being who has been crucified. When John in exile on Patmos beholds the Christ, he hears the words 'Fear not, I am the first and the last, and the living one; I died, and behold I am alive for evermore, and I have the keys of Death and Hades'.[25] In the form of the Risen Christ there is contained the human being both at earth's beginning, and at its ending; the promise and the fulfilment of his destiny on earth. In the words from Luke's Gospel Christ speaks of his flesh and his bones; and the bones are that part of the body which bear quite particularly the imprint of the Spirits of Form, preparing man for existence in a world where things have become solid, and he has to bear his own weight.

Everything in this body reveals the I. While Socrates before his death strongly distinguishes between his body and himself, the Christ can say that the disciples can see from his hands and feet 'that it is I myself'[24] (in Greek, *egō eimi autos*). Because they draw near to this body which reveals the eternal self, the redeeming of their own bodies can begin. John's Gospel says that the Christ breathed on them, and said 'Receive the Holy Spirit'.[26] The second account of man's creation in Genesis described how Yahweh 'formed man of dust from the ground, and breathed into his nostrils the breath of life; and man became a living being'.[27] Now at Easter a second process of creation begins, that man may become, as Paul says, not only a living soul but a creative spirit. The air we breathe seems formless; but all through our lives it sustains and develops our living form. Air is permeated by light; and the Christ's breath by the primordial Light in which he dwells. Receiving his breath, the disciples can begin to restore the Temple entrusted to each one of them.

5. Dynameis — the Spirits of Movement

When human beings endure great storms or destructive earthquakes, deep questions are aroused in them. The houses we build, the clothes we wear, seem to protect us enough in meeting what happens in nature through most of our lives. In many climates, the movements of nature seem for the most part friendly to man; light or strong winds, the flow of streams and rivers, the slow passage across the sky of sun and stars — in general we find them good. And if the steady earth, and the winds, suddenly appear like violent enemies of man, an anxious question stirs in the depths of his soul. What is he encountering? Is it just an external world that has always been utterly indifferent about him, which only happens, through the chance play of evolution, to be harmless and helpful for him for most of the time? Or is an enemy able to seize the elements and use them as weapons against him? Or has he to face the wrath of God? Our present world usually gives the first answer, the ancient world the second or the third.

Shakespeare was very much concerned with the effects of storms on man. *The Tempest* opens on a storm-tossed ship; Lear meets the extremity of his distress wandering through a terrible night; and perhaps the grandest storm of all is described by Pericles when his queen is in labour on board ship, to bring forth their only child.

> The god of this great vast, rebuke these surges,
> Which wash both heaven and hell; and thou that hast
> Upon the winds command, bind them in brass,
> Having called them from the deep! O, still
> Thy deaf'ning dreadful thunders: gently quench

Thy nimble sulphurous flashes. O, how, Lychorida,
How does my queen? Thou stormest venomously;
Wilt thou spit all thyself? The seaman's whistle
Is as a whisper in the ears of death,
Unheard. Lychorida — Lucina, O
Divinest patroness and midwife gentle
To those that cry by night, convey thy deity
Aboard our dancing boat; make swift the pangs
Of my queen's travails.[28]

In storm and earthquake man feels his own mortality, all
the weakness and unease of his own body. All his mastery
over nature seems very little now, before the powers let loose
around him. In a moment his individual life may end;
Pericles has soon to hear from the nurse Lychorida that
Thaisa died as their daughter was born — and Lear, after
the storm, had not long to live.

When in the far past men spoke of power, they attributed
it neither to themselves nor to a mindless external nature. It
belonged to divine beings. Men felt that it should never be
forgotten, in any surge of pride, that power is God's. When
the name of God was felt as too holy to be spoken, a word that
meant 'power' might be used to represent it.

In the Greek text of St Matthew's Gospel, in the trial
before Caiaphas, Jesus speaks of 'the right hand of Power'.[29]
The word used is *dunamis*. This is the name used by
Dionysius the Areopagite for the fifth rank of the Hierarchies, called by Rudolf Steiner the Spirits of Movement: they
are the bearers of the boundless power of God before which
man must feel his utter weakness. It is in their realm that we
have to struggle with the deepest questions about the destiny
of man.

We look at the animals. We come to the meaning of their
forms only when we see them in movement. They have
within them all the power they need for what they do, and in
their movements and in their form this is perfectly expressed.
Compared with them, man is a very clumsy creature. But the

animals have their perfect grace at the expense of universality; an animal is not in the same way as man a microcosm, a complete universe in miniature. Every animal has confined itself within a special task, and its limbs and whole form are shaped by this. Therefore the I, the individuality, does not have for the animals the same sense as for man. Particular animals and birds do have very definite qualities of their own; but the development of the everyday self into a more and more perfect servant of the greater, eternal self — often touched upon in this book — does not come about within a particular animal. Wise individualities are indeed to be found, as Rudolf Steiner has described, which use many animals of a particular kind rather as we use our fingers: a single spirit, for example, behind whole multitudes of sheep. These animal spirits are offspring of the Spirits of Movement; and the contemplation of the destiny of the animal in relation to the destiny of man can lead us far towards an understanding of this rank of the hierarchies.

The particular animal is not very wise, but it loves. What it has as wisdom belongs for the most part really to the group-spirit and is shown most in activities which are repeated over and over again, as in the shaping of cells by the bees. But a single animal can love other members of its kind and human beings — sometimes responding in very remarkable ways to particular people and situations.

Animals love; and they suffer pain. They grieve about things that happen to them, and they endure pain in their bodies as man does. And when they grieve or suffer pain they cannot look beyond the moment, as man can do, but are confined in it. They do not really know what has caused their trouble, or how long it will last. They cannot recognize, as man can do, that their pain may be the result of their own stupidity or of their own fault.

For man, the existence of pain can become a question to the universe, as the presence of storm and natural destruction can be. He can ask about the divine justice. How could a just God allow so many innocent beings to suffer?

We can try to look more attentively at pain, what it is, and how it arises. If we look at the animals, we can see that they have joy in their very existence. For the most part, this joy predominates. There is deep satisfaction in their natural activities, in food and warmth and companionship and play. Pain comes usually through the interruption or hindering of a natural activity; from hunger or thirst, cold or some kind of confinement. In its need the animal struggles — to find food or drink, to get warm, to escape. And here already we touch one of the mysteries of pain. An animal or a man can suffer without being at all clear about the cause of the pain, or about a means of alleviating it. An animal indeed never understands the cause of pain or its remedy in quite the same way as a man can do. The wisdom its whole organism incorporates can lead it to the right answer — or fail to do so. In its actual consciousness there is something like the experience man has when he dreams; the picture of what is needed may simply arise, as a man who is crippled may dream that he is walking freely. Sometimes a human being may be quite unable to interpret what his suffering is about. It is possible for a child to be hungry for quite a long time without knowing that he needs food.

Yet every pain and discomfort presses towards an answer. An animal that is attacked tries to run away, or to fight back. And in a human being the very first reaction is movement, even before the pain has been identified. But persistent distress drives us into consciousness; just as something very disastrous happening in a dream can wake us up. Then we may discover whether our distress is concerned with what we call reality or not.

It is part of the fate of the animal that he cannot quite wake up. It is merciful that his suffering is not generally very long extended in time — unless it is inflicted by man's devices, his traps and experiments. The battles of animal with animal are relatively brief. It is the group-spirit of the animal who knows what the pain of his members means in the world's household. And he is much more awake than man.

When a man is attacked, he generally responds with some kind of anger. He regards the attacking animal or man as an enemy, and evil. Later on he may come to distinguish between what seems like violence or savagery in the animal and the violence of men. An animal may feed upon other animals, or defend its territory against other members of its own kind; and in doing these things it is following the necessities of its own nature. It is a lack of understanding if we think of these things as evil. Nor is a snake evil, if it bites a man who picks it up without permission!

We do not feel responsible for what we do in dreams, unless we regard this as a true reflection of what we are like in waking life. A human being can cause another pain quite unintentionally, or even while trying to help. An action can only be called evil, with truth, when the doer intends the pain and harm he causes, and acts out of an impulse foreign to his own deepest nature. A human being who commits a real murder, the considered destruction of another person's life, has already killed something in himself. Such an action causes pain, not simply to the victim, but generally to a whole circle of people who are concerned; and this is a pain not easily understood. Very often when we suffer we can see that this is directly helpful to us, warning us about a harmful influence in our organism which could have passed unnoticed; but when a man chooses to do evil this seems nothing but tragedy.

The relationship between evil and pain is however not quite a simple one. Evil always causes pain, though not every pain can be traced to evil in any direct way: and if we try to understand the person who does evil, we may find that there is some deep suffering in the background. A man may feel that he, or people close to him, have suffered a great injustice for which there was no redress. He may feel indeed that the power responsible is continuing to act in the same unjust way. Or a man may suffer from an overwhelming desire as David does for Bathsheba, and see no way of satisfying this desire except by a terrible misdeed. Thus suffering may turn to evil where the human being sees no other way out.

When Shakespeare describes a man possessed by evil, there is often a hint of this. Richard III suffers from his misshapen form, and becomes a tyrant. Oliver in *As You Like It* suffers because others find his brother Orlando much more lovable than himself; and plans his brother's death. Iago finds his ambition frustrated by Othello; so he destroys the other's happiness and in the end several lives. And in *King Lear*, the villainies of Edmund spring from the bitter knowledge that he is a bastard. But Shakespeare is quite aware that suffering need not have this result. A human being can grow into the most radiant, most patient quality of forgiveness as does Queen Katherine in *Henry VIII*, one of the last passages Shakespeare wrote.

The mystery of evil deepens if we do not look only at animals and men, but up into spiritual realms. At the present time, many theologians think it quite childish to believe that man has spiritual adversaries. But if we recognize that there is anything at all beyond the reach of our senses there is no good reason to deny that bad powers exist as well as good ones; we see the results of their work; it can however remain deeply puzzling that such beings could come into and remain in existence, not in the physical world but in a realm of which we think that it must be filled with the divine glory. And the human heart has always asked — why are such beings allowed to have so much power? As we have tried to see, men have always believed that power belongs ultimately to God, the Almighty; why should he share this with evil beings? The New Testament actually uses the same word that stands for the godhead, *dunamis*, for the evil 'powers of the heavens'[30] with which the Christian has to fight. Long ago, the writer of the Book of Job struggles with this whole problem. He found some great answers; but they may not seem to us complete.

The Spirits of Movement work in the midst of these questions, not as matters of theory, but as powerful realities.

This may seem to contradict what has been said above, that the Third Hierarchy are concerned with leading the human soul, while the Second Hierarchy are creative beings in the world of nature and of the life-forces of man. The Spirits of Movement are indeed not limited to the concerns of the soul, but they do watch over its whole progress through the evolution of the earth, and the effect of changes within it upon the life-forces in man and in the world. It was they who long ago, before the earth yet was, stirred man to dream. In that ancient condition of things, when the Angels were passing through a stage like that of men on earth, the Spirits of Movement were already creators. (This is the condition called by Rudolf Steiner 'Old Moon'.) Throughout this time, men were in a state of consciousness comparable to that of the animals today. But there were no solid forms then; everything was in continual transformation. This changefulness alleviated the sorrows and desires to which the soul was subject. In its meeting with change, the soul can grow strong, even while it dreams.

On earth, the human soul has by no means lost all kinship with its earlier state. Even in what we call waking life, we dream a good deal. And we are not yet able to meet pain and evil with enough inner strength. On the path of spiritual development, the exercise of inner strength is a task for each individual man, with the help of those close to him. But it is also a task for humanity in general and in so far as progress is made with this, there are not only changes in man's soul, but in his 'life-body' or 'body of formative forces' as well. A mood in the soul becomes a habit in life.

Among the qualities in the soul which can become basic characteristics of the life-body there are two which have great significance in the encounter with pain and evil. They are courage and compassion; and for long ages Spirits of Movement have fostered them in man. It is not difficult to see how man is ennobled by these qualities; but it is not always understood that they could not arise in him, were pain not present in the world. We need courage to face pain, and compassion to share in the pain of others. And a still greater courage is wanted in order to meet the presence and activity of evil in the right way.

Courage and compassion both run counter to man's natural and indeed necessary inclinations. We want to avoid pain; were this not so, pain would be ineffective as a warning about harm that threatens our bodies. But courage accepts the likelihood of pain, for the sake of a purpose that is to be achieved. And compassion impels us to share sufferings which it would be possible to avoid. It is natural too for man to wish for a world in which evil was not present. But his service of great purposes would have less meaning, if he did not have to meet enemies on the way. He need not hate these enemies; to them too compassion can extend, when we begin to recognize the origin of evil in suffering, and that to live in evil is a kind of suffering too. For evil is obsession, which means a state of siege. The soul may find, for instance, that impulses of jealousy assail it from every side, and that it is unable to move on into any other mood. Hatred for another person can infect all our seeing, all our doing. It is easy to blame someone who is caught in such feelings. But it is much more useful to have compassion for him. This is one of the ways in which Shakespeare shows himself a man of the future, that those figures in his plays who are obsessed by an evil mood — Shylock, Macbeth, Leontes — gradually win our compassion; though Shakespeare does not forget that evil is a reality.

An obsession is a loss of movement. Yet it can be active in destruction, like a sorely wounded animal. The obsessed man can only be helped by tranquillity and action combined in quite another way; by inner peace. Where this is truly present, there is no inactivity, and no disturbance. If we can imagine this as a quality, not just within and around a human soul, but working with cosmic majesty in sun and planets, we may reach out in feeling towards the Spirits of Movement.

There are moments in the history of mankind when

through a single personality, or a group of people, great gates open, through which the influence of spirits of the Hierarchies can stream. Rudolf Steiner has described how this happened in the life of Gautama Buddha. What poured through him as a most far-reaching influence had its source in one of the Spirits of Movement, the inspirer of compassion. This was the Spirit of Movement who is connected with one of the inner planets, Mercury, the swiftly altering herald of sunset and dawn. While European man was principally developing the mood of courage, expressed in martial valour, Eastern man received the gentle and peaceful teachings about a way of action which would harm no living thing. Not immediately following Buddha's coming, but from a few centuries later, countless representations of his form were made; looking at these, men saw at first a great tranquillity, a stillness undisturbed by any shadow of unrest. And yet movement originates in this stillness; a movement that touches and includes every pain and grief with its tenderness and hope. The Buddha does not work only for those who look upon his image. Souls who have been inspired by him carry his influence into civilizations which may not even have heard his name. Souls of this kind are among those best able to understand the Christ as healer of mankind. It is from this point of view that Luke, the evangelist, always describes the Christ; as the bringer of a forgiveness able to restore human beings to the household of God.

In Luke's understanding, Buddhism and Christianity flow together. But European man cannot at first prepare his soul for the depths of this compassion. Through the centuries, men and women appear here and there who reveal it in their actions; St Columba on Iona, St Elizabeth at Marburg, St Francis in Italy. In each of these exceptional courage grows into all-inclusive compassion. In many of the stories told about them, animals play a special part; it is as if they begin to recognize in these men and women the promise that their long sorrows will end.

It is one of the most encouraging signs of our own times that when disaster strikes in any part of the world a compassionate response seems to come so quickly from almost everywhere. We seem to have gone a long way towards learning that there is no human suffering which does not concern us. And much compassion goes out to the animals too; though an enormous amount of their suffering under experimentation or in 'factory farming' is hidden from general notice. But we often lack the courage which is needed to express compassion in action; in small and great matters, we hesitate out of conventionality or out of fear. While in our time there are many extraordinary acts of personal courage and endurance, we have a very widespread fear of bodily pain and of the soul's grief. And there is a lack of courage which is still more universal; a submission to the fear of encounter with spiritual realities. This has long been present in humanity; when he appears in vision to John, Christ has to say, even to so great a man: 'Fear not'. It is particularly between adolescence and the middle twenties that many people today are having sudden encounters with spiritual experience — and the shock and bewilderment can be very great.

The strengthening of our powers of courage and compassion needs to be undertaken today quite consciously as part of the path of spiritual development. In the deepest inner quietness we can achieve, we have to try to prepare ourselves for events and encounters that are to come, and will call for our active response. We need to recognize, not just as an idea in our minds, but as a habitual feeling, that a danger is not made any worse by being seen for what it is. We need to feel again and again in meditation that spiritual beings and events are just as real as, and indeed more real than is the visible world around us. When we enter the world of spirit after leaving the body at death, it will not be something quite strange to us, but a familiar home to which we are returning, though we had so often forgotten it. And incidents that may seem strange and terrifying by themselves are parts of things which would have meaning if experienced as a whole; as a shadow at the door may startle us before we recognize our friend.

In all this we draw near to the realm of the Spirits of Movement. They wish to lead further the soul which once was sunk in dreams. In the physical world it awakens; and it has to prepare for all that will be asked of it, in order to awake beyond the physical world. Beyond death, we shall feel more deeply with others, and endure encounters stranger than we have ever done here — although these feelings and encounters only bring us back, in the last resort, to things which are part of ourselves.

In wonderful ways, some of the arts can help us with all this. We look at all the graces of movement which are to be found among the animals — creeping, pacing, fluttering, swimming, leaping — and feel in ourselves the endless variety of significant movement of which we are capable. In all times of our history, the dance has been one of the wonders of life and a bridge between the visible and the invisible. In our time a new art of movement, the eurythmy brought into being under Rudolf Steiner's guidance, adds to poetry and music a rich language of the arms and feet. Both the seeing of such movements and the performing of them, can have a healing effect. We find ourselves again in the many-sidedness of our being.

We have tried to see that evil is a failure in movement; a refusal to accept and accomplish a necessary change. Evil acts out of a past it will not leave behind, or a future snatched before the necessary growth towards it. It needs to be brought back into the measured paces of the great dance.

6. Kyriotetes — the Spirits of Wisdom

Only gradually does it become evident to us, that very familiar things are great mysteries. Waking and sleeping, breathing and eating — we are very disinclined to accept that such things, which we have been doing all our lives, remain deeply mysterious to us. We may have accumulated a great deal of scientific knowledge, and then added spiritual knowledge as well; if we have understood what has been learned, our questions about simple things become greater, not less. We look out at the world in its wonderful variety; we watch sheep grazing in a field, or deer coming over the brow of a hill, and unfathomable mysteries are presented to us. We look at our own faces in a mirror; and we see the image of an eye that looks at its own image. We do not know how this can be; the questions we need to ask lead out to the limits of the universe, and back again. To achieve real knowledge, we would have to transform ourselves; and this is what mystery means — a task for the understanding, which can only be approached through the transformation of thought, and feeling, and will.

Looking at animals and plants, we are confronted by the mystery of their difference. In the stillness of a great forest, we can listen for any movement of an animal — feeling the slow growth of a tree or even the smallest flower, and the anxious alertness, the swift responses, of a rabbit or a mouse. What we see of tree or flower, of beast or bird, is incomplete; were we to seek the rest of what belongs essentially to each, we would have to enter different worlds.

There is a wonderful passage in Genesis which can illuminate this. Abraham is returning from a long journey, on which he has rescued his kinsman Lot from enemies.

And Melchizedek king of Salem brought out bread and wine; he was priest of God Most High. And he blessed him and said,
> 'Blessed be Abram by God Most High,
>> maker of heaven and earth;
> And blessed be God Most High
>> who has delivered your enemies into your hand!'

And Abram gave him a tenth of everything.[31]

Here in a few words a very significant meeting is described. Both Abraham and Melchizedek are representatives of a holy wisdom, but they have different tasks. When Abraham brings an offering to the God he serves, it is an animal. Melchizedek's offering is bread and wine — and this Abraham recognizes as something that is higher. When a man of the ancient world brought a true offering, it became transparent for him; he looked through it into the spiritual world without which it was incomplete. He did not claim it any longer as his own earthly possession; he looked into the holy wisdom from which it came, and which should have dominion over it for ever. Earlier in Genesis, Abel brings the sacrifice of the animal, and it is accepted; Cain tries to bring an offering of 'the fruit of the ground', and does not find acceptance.[32] What is meant here is no triviality; it is a question of how man can perform actions which reconcile heaven and earth.

In the animal sacrifice there was a deep humility. Man felt himself not very far removed from the animals' dreaming consciousness. His soul too was driven by fears and desires, unable to take hold of what was happening with steady understanding. He had seized the fruit of the tree of knowledge of good and evil before he was ready to use it well. Offering the animal, which did not presume to have wisdom as its own possession, he sought the shepherding spirit outside himself. And the divine will responds to this humility.

If on the other hand he is to bring the pure offering which

comes from the wheat and from the vine, he must have something in himself which matches this purity. He must have made knowledge sufficiently part of himself not to feel any pride about its possession, although it makes him like a god. He must feel how an immortal self shines down into him from the heights of the world, just as the flowering fields of earth reflect the starry meadows of the sky.

In Cain, this is not yet achieved. He has seized the future without being prepared for it; and he has the terrible fate of becoming the first murderer. In Melchizedek the immortal being has awakened; he is not just the child of an earthly family. The Letter to the Hebrews refers to this. Melchizedek 'is without father or mother or genealogy, and has neither beginning of days nor end of life but resembling the Son of God he continues a priest for ever'.[33]

Melchizedek appears only for a moment in the Old Testament record. The mystery of bread and wine is revealed again with the coming of Christ. Now the offering is brought by the one who unites in himself the Tree of Knowledge and the Tree of Life, who is entirely selfless in his knowing and living. Melchizedek is king of Salem, that is, king of peace. At the Last Supper, Christ gives his peace to the disciples; 'not as the world gives do I give to you'[34]. Through the Christ, men receive a share in the realm beyond all conflict, the tranquil heavenly order. The bread and wine become transparent for the highest hierarchies of the spirit.

The animal has on earth a physical body, a life-body, and the bearer of joys and wishes and griefs — what is called the astral body. In the nearest region of the invisible there dwells the wise individuality of the species. The plant has here only physical body and life-body. It is only gently touched by an astral body which belongs in the same realm as the animal group-spirit. There are great group-spirits of the plants as well, of which countless particular plants are the members; and these work on a higher level of being, which is only reached by the human soul some considerable time after death. These group-spirits can truly be called heavenly beings, though they are deeply concerned with the fate of the earth. They are the offspring of the Spirits of Wisdom, the rank of beings above the Spirits of Movement, and are the highest rank of the Second Hierarchy. They receive their creative wisdom from the First Hierarchy — the Seraphim, Cherubim and Thrones — and weave it into all the life of the solar system. We may feel something of the greatness of the sun by turning first towards the Spirits of Form, through whom all visible things strive towards their archtypes, towards the Spirits of Movement, through whom all beings meet and part, passing through need and fulfilment, and towards the Spirits of Wisdom, who give all things their meaning, their place within the whole.

Shakespeare tried often to give some picture in his plays of this realm beyond conflict. In *King Lear* the night of bewilderment is peopled by wild and suffering animals; in the morning Lear comes into meadows where he can make himself a crown of wild flowers. In *Macbeth* we have side by side the tyrant who compared himself to a chained bear and the true king who is described as sovereign flower, healing his country. And earlier in the play we have the picture which recurs in Shakespeare — the banquet, in which Macbeth as murderer cannot share. Through the presence of Banquo's ghost, the supper is broken up and the guests are bidden to leave in a way forgetful of their rank, without any attempt at order. In *The Tempest* strange figures from another world set a banquet before 'three men of sin', and take it away before they can share in it. Each of the three has taken part in a crime or had murderous intentions. In *Henry VIII* heavenly spirits appear in vision to Queen Katherine, inviting her to a banquet in which she is found worthy to share. The experience of this vision stands in contrast with the graceless, unheralded entrance of a messenger from the earthly court.

Shakespeare is often concerned about the need for order among men, and the tragic shattering of all such order by ambition and jealousy. A community threatened with the loss of order and justice he pictures as an unweeded garden. When trees and flowers have each their right place and stature, something of the peace of Eden is won; and so it is with human communities.

At the Last Supper, a community of twelve lives in the uttermost tension between disruption and harmony. Each one is carried in Christ's loving will. And each feels himself desperately unworthy, nearly a betrayer. Each is alone, and yet united with the others. Miraculously, Leonardo da Vinci has represented this moment. The twelve are varied in appearance, and agitated in movement; and yet the picture as a whole gives an impression of unity, even of tranquillity. Peace and the acceptance of destiny stream out from the figure of Christ, and from the beloved disciple, John, who is on his right side. It can be felt that the disciples will before long achieve a sense of community in the service of Christ, though they have first to go through much bewilderment and even despair. So Christ foretells that during the approaching hours of his arrest and Passion they will be scattered. He is able to say to them 'I am the true vine, and you are the branches'. During the period that follows the Incarnation, the great teacher of community in the service of Christ is Paul. Once more, this has its beginning in an encounter that comes about where the innocent world of the plants is revealed in its wonder. Paul comes down from the desert hills into the gracious and fertile region around Damascus. With a soul full of anger, he meets the peaceful, questioning form of Christ. From this meeting there grows in him the power to draw people together in devoted communities, in which each individual has his special place. According to an ancient tradition, it was at Damascus that Cain murdered Abel. And now from Damascus a great power of reconciliation is to go forth, join together the estranged, the Jew and the Gentile, the slave and the master, the young and the old. Paul sees this great community of reconciliation in the image of the olive tree, into which branches that have been cut off can be grafted back. For long ages — in the Bible, back to the time following the flood — the olive has been taken as a sign of peace after storm.

The early Christians sometimes represented the mystery of their community in a wreath of plant forms — roses, ears of wheat, grapes and olives. If we try to contemplate these four forms of the plant, and their significance for human beings, they may help us to grow in our feeling for the Spirits of Wisdom as awakeners of a right sense for community. In each of them we see in a particular way how in the plant heavenly and earthly forces meet in wonderful harmony. Within the plant itself, this meeting is experienced in a consciousness even dimmer than that of dream; the plant is asleep, as we are when we pass beyond the realm of dreams. In the plant's sleep and the deep sleep of a human being, a harmony with the great universe is achieved which is seldom found in dreams or ordinary waking. But both in the experience of compassion, as has been described in connection with the Spirits of Movement, and in the experience of working together in a community, in which we may be helped by the Spirits of Wisdom, something like a further level of wakefulness is to be reached.

In the fragrance of a rose is to be felt what the world once was, when the Spirits of Wisdom had unfolded their creative power to the full, but nothing had yet descended to the watery or solid conditions of existence. The world was in the main light-filled air; goodness and generosity worked everywhere, inspired by happy wisdom. If we think of a rose garden, the air warm and fragrant, the sunlight clear, but not dazzling or burning; and children there playing — this mood pervaded Old Sun. On earth we achieve it only imperfectly; but just as a human being who has had a very happy early childhood may be sustained by it all through life, so the Archangels, as we have tried to see, can look back on this, their cosmic childhood, and be sustained by it. Thus they have a special kinship with the Spirits of Wisdom, as the Angels have with the Spirits of Movement. The Archangels inspire particular communities, or nations, or the shorter periods in the development of civilization. From the Spirits of Wisdom we can draw inspiration for the development of true, conscious community in general. Through the rose, they speak to us not only of the goodness of the past, but of a goodness to be achieved in the far future when a love that makes no claims and feels no jealousy will prevail in the human soul. Past and future meet in warmth and light for the present, for a community which receives the goodness of God into a grateful heart, becoming itself a rose.

In wheat, and the cereals in general, we have forms of the plant which are concerned above all with light-filled air. On their slender stems, they try to leave behind the heaviness of water and earth, taking up only a little of the finest substances. Floating in the sun-illumined air, they prepare man's bread. The cereals are transformed grasses; and they lead us back to a time when men could develop them with great wisdom and patience under the inspiration of the ancient teacher, Zarathustra. Bread sustains particularly the nervous system of man, which bears the special imprint of the Spirits of Wisdom, just as the bones do that of the Spirits of Form, or the muscles that of the Spirits of Movement. In calling men to develop the cereals, Zarathustra was thus preparing for the gradual development of man's conscious understanding, his awakening to earthly tasks. This too is part of the way in which a community finds itself; in learning to transform what is wild and disordered into gentleness and order — or simply to help what still gives little to give much.

The vine might seem to work almost in the opposite direction. It might seem fit to destroy consciousness rather than to enhance it — has it not done so, from the time when it made Noah drunk up to the present? Alcohol of every sort dulls the sensitivity of all our perceptions whether of the outer world, or of a moral or aesthetic kind. The vine itself is a bearer of warmth rather than a bearer of light; it clings close to the earth and its fruit ripens mainly not through the sun's light or its direct warmth but through warmth reflected from the earth. But the story of Noah's drunkenness really indicates a kind of experiment made by an initiate; how is this gift of the sun's warmth, transformed in earthly darkness best to be used? Through the centuries, the mystery centres watch over the use of wine, finding it a help in bringing to earth not only man's wakening perception and understanding, but his feelings and his will. He has to forget for a time his origin in the spirit, and become deeply attached to the physical body. He will find community through this, through tribe and land. But this must not go too far, or heaven's light would be lost altogether.

At the Last Supper, Christ speaks of himself as 'the true vine'. One of the interpretations of the Greek word for truth, *alētheia*, is 'unforgetting'. When Christ unites himself with the warmth of the earth, he does not forget the heavens. It is always clear to him whence he comes and whither he is going. And yet he is filled with love for the earth and for the physical body. When his communities are faithful to him, they will continue in this love.

The olive too has a remarkable place in history. The Athenians feel it as particularly their tree, the gift of their goddess, Athene. Of course it is much older than Greek civilization; but it comes here to a certain climax in its significance. Its oil has long been used in anointing, for the healing of the sick or the dedication of kings and priests. What is hard and rough, in this world of solids, it allows to move smoothly again: and its inner significance is akin to this external function. The thoughts of a king or priest need to be many-sided and mobile; they should be able to prevent friction. The olive in its silvery grey and its gnarled limbs has the look of old age, as the donkey has among the animals. Its oil can help in the passage from earth into the spiritual world.

The priest, anointed with oil, has a task inherited from the ancient mysteries, though he is not an initiate. He has to bring forth bread and wine in the spirit of Melchizedek, through the power of the community, not through his own power. He can make bread and wine transparent for the light and warmth of the spiritual sun, he can himself use the oil to help those near to the threshold of death, because the members of his community feel the Christ within them as their redeemer.

Leaders in community, who carry out in some ways the functions of kings or priests should help individual people with whom they are concerned to find their right places in the whole body; to be, as Paul describes, contented eyes, or hands, or feet. A really selfless wisdom is needed for this. No man should claim this as his own; it can only grow, as a grace bestowed on him. But there is a teaching to which he can turn, directed to those willing to seek this grace. It is the Sermon on the Mount, as we find it in Matthew's Gospel. This Gospel has indeed a special relationship to the Spirits of Wisdom, as the other three Gospels have to the three ranks of the First Hierarchy. It is the Gospel that tells of the wise men from the East, who bring their three offerings to the Child at Bethlehem. It describes how this child is taken, to escape Herod's violence, to the ancient land of wisdom, Egypt. And it contains an abundance of teaching given particularly to the disciples, as future teachers and leaders in congregations. Many difficulties in understanding the Sermon on the Mount can be overcome, if it is remembered that it is spoken to those preparing themselves for such responsibilities, and not simply to Christians in general. Every word needs to be tested, both in its immediate context and the great context of human responsibility.

How many readers of the Gospels in modern languages must have been discouraged by the words: 'You, therefore, must be perfect, as your heavenly Father is perfect'.[35] The Greek word rendered 'perfect' is *teleios* which has also the meanings 'complete' and 'fit for its purpose'; it is the quality a sacrificial animal must have, of being free from blemish. The context here shows that what is meant is not that the disciples should be free from blemish in the sense of having no faults — for they are to be taught very soon to acknowledge their faults, in the Lord's Prayer — but that the love and understanding they give to their congregations should not be partial, preferring one kind of people to other kinds but going out to all. This is a responsibility which belongs to the vocation they are accepting. One might almost call it a professional responsibilty; just as we expect a doctor or a nurse to give equal care to a disagreeable patient or a judge not to favour his friends.

There is much else in the Sermon on the Mount that can be seen in this light. The Magi can rightly be called 'wise men'; but it cannot be said without reserve of the disciples that they are either wise or good. None the less the very first sentences of the Sermon on the Mount describe them and give Christ's blessing on them, as beggars for the spirit and people who hunger and thirst for justice. But they are not to seek justice for themselves by retaliation, while they are guiding a community; as a teacher or a mental nurse, for example, may not simply permit himself to hit back at a child or a patient. He must think first of what is needed by the one who has injured him.

Wisdom teaches that everyone is to be included, that everyone has a necessary place in a community. It is very easy to see this in principle, very difficult to carry it out effectively in practice. We are caught up in countless likes and dislikes. But the task itself teaches us.

The First
Hierarchy

7. Thrones, Cherubim and Seraphim

The difficulties of reaching out in human understanding, and describing in human speech, culminate with the First Hierarchy. There are two particular reasons for this. One of them deeply concerned Dionysius; these beings are very close to the inexpressible being of the Godhead, and all human words must falter because of this. The other reason is new. Without the First Hierarchy, there would be no physical world; Rudolf Steiner makes this clear, and something of the same shines through the words of Dionysius. But in our time, the physicists' conception of matter stands in the way. It is an unsatisfying conception from many points of view; and yet we are persuaded that it must have something to do with reality, for it works, with the most terrible effectiveness. If their strange theory of a multitude of particles which are not particles, but rather changes in something which is in no ordinary sense a thing — if this represents accurately by the nature of the physical world, what place is there for the First Hierarchy in it? Immense energies, which can long be dormant yet when released can be destructive beyond anything man had imagined before — this picture is very difficult to reconcile with a goodness at the foundation of things. And it works. The physicist arranges for these immense energies to be released, by means of fantastically delicate and complex devices — and they are released. To take what may seem a trivial picture; it is as if a mother left all sorts of poisons, explosives, and sharp instruments in a room where her small children were playing alone. God seems to have left dangerous stuff lying about everywhere.

Of course similar questions about suffering and evil have

long pressed on the mind of man. And many have tried to explain, more stumblingly or more effectively that without pain man's soul would not learn, and that without the possibility of evil man could not be free; but what conceivable need was there, to put it very crudely, to make matter such a dangerous thing? Perhaps behind this problem as well there is something essential for man to learn.

Again and again in considering the hierarchies, we are led towards the question: what is reality? The English word 'real' goes back to the Latin word *res*, a thing. Those with languages close to Latin are thus taught, without particularly noticing it, that reality is a matter of things; while the Dutch or German words link reality with working, with effectiveness. Probably the majority of human beings all over the world think of reality as concerned with physical facts and processes. And yet this leaves out of account that all our ideas of external facts are taken from what somebody perceives or somebody thinks — that is to say, from events in *consciousness*, not simply in space and time. What would a thing be, if it had no consciousness, and no one perceived or understood it? It might as well not be! We can conceive of reality far better as composed of conscious beings, their activities and relationships.

We spend a great part of our lives dealing with material objects which seem to be quite unconscious. But the whole tenor of this book has been that this is an illusion. May we not expect that a stone or a human artefact could become transparent in the same way that a living plant can, revealing to us worlds of creative beings?

Before trying to answer this, perhaps we should look carefully at the effects that time spent in dealing with material objects can have on us. On the one hand, this schools us in the recognition of what we are actually doing. The car moves as we steer it, the cake comes out as we made it. Where complex technologies are being used, a very fine sense of responsibility may develop. Care or the lack of it in the use of material things may have far-reaching effects.

On the other hand, a feeling may grow up that material objects, experiencing no joy or pain, are entirely replaceable; that it may not matter in the least, for instance, how much is thrown away. A man may set his whole mind on an aim he wishes to achieve, and may regard the things used on the way with indifference.

It can easily be seen that a disregard for materials may lead to a disregard for people, and care about materials lead to care for people. Very often indeed, we are concerned with both; for a material thing generally represents someone's work and someone's possession. But we like to think that every object can be replaced, while we know that no person can.

It is as if the material world put a great question to us: 'How will you use me?' If one believes that there is no questioner, one may become a destroyer. A great awe can grow up in anyone who believes that he is indeed being questioned by what seem to be the lifeless things in the world. He may come to say: mighty and noble are the spiritual beings who stand behind the animal and behind the growing plant — but I would have to seek even further, and feel an even deeper reverence, were I to seek the beings whose patience and sacrifice make possible the realm of lifeless things.

In the names for the hierarchies used by Dionysius the Areopagite, those from the Spirits of Wisdom down to the Angels have a certain similarity. The Greek words, Kyriotetes, Dynameis, Exousiai, Archai, all suggest authority and power; Angelos means messenger. For the First Hierarchy we have two Hebrew names, Seraphim and Cherubim, and one that is Greek, Thrones, which is perhaps the most enigmatic name of all nine. It is never used in the Bible explicitly as a rank of spiritual beings. When it appears, it is usually in the singular, as the throne of God. It could be asked 'Why should spiritual beings be called after an inanimate thing, a human artefact?' It appears with an extraordinary emphasis in the Revelation to John: 'At once I was in the Spirit, and lo, a throne stood in heaven, with one seated on the throne!'[36] In Isaiah this emphasis is not present in the same way 'I saw the Lord sitting upon a throne, high and lifted up'.[37]

If we read several chapters of the Revelation to John consecutively, there often seem to be abrupt changes of mood and theme. But if we look more closely, we may find that what follows has been prepared in some way, perhaps quite unobtrusively. Here the great vision of the throne in heaven has been prepared in the last of the seven letters to the churches. At the end of each letter a promise is given to the members of each congregation of what will be fulfilled if they are victorious over the adversary powers. To the members of the church at Laodicea it is said: 'He who conquers, I will grant him to sit with me on my throne, as I myself conquered and sat down with my Father on his throne.'[38] John takes this promise deeply into his heart, and it prepares him for the open door in heaven, for the divine throne in the midst, and for the twenty-four thrones of the elders around it.

What are thrones, and what are they doing in the spiritual world? Every chair we sit on is one of their come-down descendants. In ancient times ordinary people did not sit in chairs, they stood or reclined, or sat on the ground, or at the most sat on some kind of bench. To sit on a separate chair was to be like a king, and when a king sat he was like a god! A subject, looking towards one whom he saw as a true king seated upon his throne, felt himself included in a steady vision, a warm acceptance, and an active, merciful will. The Greek work *thronos* is akin to the Latin *firmus* from which such English words as firm and affirm come (and the beautiful word, confirmation) and to the Sanskrit *dharma* the expression of cosmic law. The essential thing about a throne or chair is that it does sustain, showing that faithful reliability for which we can be so grateful in inanimate things — sustains a being who is fully awake. There is something disturbing about an animal sitting on a chair, and even about a human being sleeping in a chair; a sort of armchair known as a 'shepherd's chair' used to be made which upset its occupant if he fell asleep.

Rudolf Steiner's name for the beings Dionysius calls Thrones is 'Spirits of Will'. We have to think, not of any arbitrary will, but of the utmost patience and steadfastness. Behind everything in the world that is calculable and regular we can think of a sustaining purpose which accepts a sacrifice. Beings who once created spontaneously, in a way that could not be calculated, have for long ages put aside this freedom; one day they will resume it. Their sacrifice is for the sake of other beings, who need a calculable world. In the sacrifice, the Father's will is put into effect.

Just as the whole Third Hierarchy can be thought of as the instrument of the Holy Spirit, and the whole Second Hierarchy as revealing the glory of the Son God, so the whole First Hierarchy works in the immediate service of the Father God. This may help us to understand what otherwise may seem strange in John's description of the heavenly throne, 'And he who sat there appeared like jasper and carnelian, and round the throne was a rainbow that looked like an emerald'.[39] In attempting to describe the very highest, to which human thought can reach, John makes a comparison with stones. As in the account of the New Jerusalem, he uses the names of what we call precious and semi-precious stones; some of them are transparent, and some opaque, but, in a more far-reaching sense, for him they are all transparent. He looks through the stones to mighty individualities, as we should try to look through the animals and the plants to their group-spirits. The mighty individualities of the stones are the offspring of the Spirits of Will. Colours of flower and leaf glow forth and pass away; the red of the carnelian, the green of the emerald, endure as long as the earth.

It is not because of their beauty or scarcity alone that certain stones have been regarded as precious. They have been felt as the bearers of certain moral qualities; the name amethyst, for example, means something free from intoxication, bringing a pure consciousness. Anyone can wear a jewel; and in the Revelation of St John the great harlot Babylon is described as 'bedecked with gold and jewels and pearls'.[40] But this is a kind of blasphemy; the wearer or user of gold or jewels should recognize their holiness and be purified by it. It is not for nothing that Shakespeare speaks of 'sermons in stones'; the rocks of earth preach to man of tasks reaching through long ages of time, during which what is dark and confused in the depths of his being should achieve the translucence of a crystal.

Colet sums up the description of the First Hierarchy by Dionysius in the words: 'Power cleanses, clear truth makes serene, finished love makes perfect'.[41] The power is that of the Thrones, the clear truth that of the Cherubim, the finished love that of the Seraphim. He does not mean that they have power, or truth, or love as their own separate possession; they share, more than any other beings, in the power and truth and love of God. Before the First Hierarchy, man has to face what the ultimate purification of his being means. He must face the complete rejection of every trace of untruthfulness. In the Garden of Eden, and again by the river in the New Jerusalem, the Tree of Life stands: but no-one may come to it who 'loves and practises falsehood'.[42] In Genesis it is said 'At the east of the garden of Eden he placed the cherubim, and a flaming sword which turned every way, to guard the way to the tree of life'.[43]

We do not lie only by misrepresenting external facts, but because in our words the true essences of things are not brought to life. If a human being does share to some extent in the wonders of the spiritual world, he longs to tell his fellow men about them. But the language he uses on earth is unfit for the task. He is unworthy to be a messenger of the spirit in the whole bearing of his soul, and in all the habits of his life. He has to say something like the confession of Isaiah: 'Woe is me! For I am lost; for I am a man of unclean lips, and I dwell in the midst of a people of unclean lips; for my eyes have seen the King, the LORD of hosts!' Isaiah then receives a healing grace, from the realm even higher than that of the Cherubim. 'Then flew one of the seraphim to me, having in his hand a burning coal which he had taken with tongs from the altar. And he touched my mouth, and said: "Behold, this has touched your lips; your guilt is taken away, and your sin forgiven." And I heard the voice of the Lord saying, "Whom shall I send, and who will go for us?" Then I said, "Here I am! Send me." '44

What is it that has made man's speech unclean? What is it that has dragged down our words and made them unlike the creative Logos, of which they are images? It is evident that this fall has been brought about in part by human emotions. Speech has been darkened by anger, jealousy and fear. It has been corrupted too from outside, because we have used it to describe external things in tones forgetful of their divine origin. The Revelation to John describes how the merchants who bewail Babylon remember all the things bought and sold there, and include the bodies and souls of men. The speech of the market place is debased indeed from both sides; by desire from within, by idolatry from without. For idolatry as it is meant in the Old and New Testament extends to all overprizing of what can be possessed on earth.

Speech then has to be purified. Fire from the altar can do this. From the holiest realm the Seraphim bring burning, glowing love. Through this we discover what we really desire, and what things really are. Isaiah feels in a moment the deep change in him, and he is ready to become a messenger. For most of us, such changes come about very slowly; we ripen, as the harvest does, but over many years and lifetimes.

Shakespeare is very much aware of the mysterious power of the years to bring about maturity. Of course this does not happen inevitably; in Polonius he has shown, in a way more terrible than is often realized, how old age can live in illusions, and superficiality masquerade as wisdom. No real growing is without pain. In *King Lear* there are two old men who grow, and overcome some of their illusions. One of them, the Duke of Gloucester, is robbed of the sight of his physical eyes by a violent deed. His son Edgar has lost place and possessions through a cruel trick. As a ragged beggar he has feigned madness. For him as well as for his father, death seems not far off. And he says to his father:

> Men must endure
> Their going hence, even as their coming hither;
> Ripeness is all.[45]

Edgar brings together the mysteries of birth and death. Both can be seen as profound changes in our relationship to the First Hierarchy. At birth we enter the physical world — we come among things. It can puzzle a baby for quite a time to meet objects which are neither loving nor angry however he treats them. Deep within him is a profound awe; and sometimes we catch a glimpse, particularly with a very young child, of the rich experience he brings with him. And where human beings have not lost awe, or have found it again, old age may bring them a little nearer to the realm of Seraphim, Cherubim and Thrones. Through this approach an aged human being can reveal something of the character of this realm. In a wonderful passage about the ascent of the soul through the hierarchies, Rudolf Steiner says that there are some old people whose words convey something of the serene wisdom of the Cherubim — not simply through the wisdom of their speech, but more by its mood and quality. And there are some old people whose very presence, without it being necessary for them to speak or act, can bring us a feeling for the Seraphim.

It is said that when he was very old John the Evangelist often used to say: 'Little children, love one another!' Such words would have had quite a different effect, if they had been spoken by someone else. Through long patience and endurance, through years of unassuming work in the congregations of Asia, and through pondering his memories of the years with Jesus Christ during his earthly ministry, John had achieved a maturity which gave his words their special music. All through his Gospel it is to be heard. It lifts us up into the boundless light of the Cherubim, a wisdom to be reached by Angels rather than by men. And yet there is a wonderful attentiveness to physical detail in John's Gospel, as an eagle's vision can survey wide horizons and pick out small movements on the ground. The Samaritan woman leaves her vessel by the well when she goes to fetch her friends; Jesus girds himself with a towel before he washes the feet of his disciples. And the Gospel is very much concerned with the encounters between Christ Jesus and particular human beings. Yet through John's words there always resounds the wisdom of eternity.

Of St Luke's Gospel, Rudolf Steiner says that it leads us into the realm of the Seraphim. It is the Gospel of glowing, sacrificial love. There is a being with whom both St John and St Luke have much to do, of whose words we have very little record in the New Testament, but whose presence must have brought an unforgettable blessing: Mary, the mother of Jesus. St Luke is sometimes represented as painting her portrait; for tradition describes him as a painter as well as a physician. It is St Luke who tells of her presence among the Apostles after the Ascension. Through her whole life she must have brought fathomless comfort to the Apostles when they returned from the trials of their long journeys. From this seraphic warmth Luke could draw, when he told Christ's parables of forgiveness, and described his healing deeds.

In St Mark's Gospel we meet the impact of an unfailing will. St Mark has a particular relationship to the realm of the Thrones, perhaps because he had himself experienced a faltering of the will, in the way described in the Acts of the Apostles. He had turned back, when Paul and Barnabas journeyed on, into the interior of Asia Minor. He had become the interpreter of Peter, the apostle in whom there was on the one hand such a gigantic power of will, but also sudden moments of acute weakness. And at the last Mark could face undaunted the hostility of a city which had become profoundly materialistic, and there suffer his own martyrdom. His Gospel is the shortest of the four; almost everything in it is to be found in Matthew or in Luke as well. Everything in Mark is described with a clear directness which shows the power of Christ's will to accomplish his task. Not much of teaching, not much of parable, but action upon action, bearing heavenly will into the life of the fallen earth.

St Matthew's Gospel shows in Jesus Christ a wise harmony of human qualities, by which the disciples can be led towards responsibility. Mark, Luke and John bring before us a strength of purpose, a loving kindness, and a heavenly wisdom which are more than human — yet in their presence man's thinking, feeling and willing can ripen into maturity. Only in this way can he hope to overcome the materialism which threatens to take him prisoner.

How can the physical world be a manifestation of the First Hierarchy, and yet bring such danger to the human soul? We should not demand that an explanation of the physical world must be very simple; even a purely quantitative description of familiar material processes soon becomes very complex. In the Book of Ezekiel there is a description of the Cherubim in which there is some indication of the riddles in this realm, and of ways towards answering them. First Ezekiel describes the four living creatures themselves; their faces, their wings, their bodies and their movements. And then he describes the wheels that follow them, their movements corresponding to the movements of the Cherubim themselves.

When they went, they went in any of their four directions without turning as they went. The four wheels had rims and they had spokes; and their rims were full of eyes round about. And when the living creatures went, the wheels went beside them; and when the living creatures rose from the earth, the wheels rose. Wherever the spirit would go, they went, and the wheels rose along with them; for the spirit of the living creatures was in the wheels. When those went, these went; and when those stood, these stood; and when those rose from the earth, the wheels rose along with them; for the spirit of the living creatures was in the wheels.[46]

Among human artefacts, the wheel has a special place. Tools are generally an extension of what human limbs can already do, and in some way resemble the forms of the limbs. But in our immediate natural environment, in stone and plant and animal, and in the physical body of man, there are no wheels. When men began to give their vehicles wheels, they were doing something very surprising indeed. They had not seen a wheel anywhere in the physical world. Much had to be changed, to make environments suitable for wheels. And very much more could be changed, by means of the wheels we made.

When Ezekiel looks at wheels in his vision they are very different. The spirit of the living creatures is in them; and their rims are full of eyes. In human machinery spirit is used in the construction and arrangement of the wheels; but it is not in them, and they have no eyes. They take time to turn; but the time has no meaning for them. Strange as it may sound, this is the tragedy of our technology. It works in space, using time as if it had no meaning.

Like the other ranks of the hierarchies, the Cherubim and Seraphim have offspring. These work in the rhythms of time. All the life of plant and animal on earth is interwoven, in a very complex and mysterious way, with the rhythms of time; the elemental beings, offspring of the Third Hierarchy, respond to the guidance of the offspring of the First Hierarchy, the spirits of day and month and year. *Their* movement is full of meaning, warmed and illumined from the very springs of all existence.

Every rhythm turns, coming back to where it was before, perhaps not completely, but in some way that can be recognized; as with a wheel that goes along a road, a point on the rim is sometimes above the hub and sometimes below, and yet moves on. A significant rhythm sets forth with love, and returns with love, irradiated at every point of its changing course by wisdom. Night hungers for day, day thirsts for the night. During our life on earth, something in us reaches out towards our home in the spiritual world; during our life in heaven, our courage mounts to meet the earth once more. As the human soul matures, it learns to accept more and more every changing condition of its existence.

But there are spiritual powers who oppose the offspring of the First Hierarchy. They try to empty both time and space of all their meaning. The kind of maturity which would be developed under their influence would be utterly different from what has been described: it would be intensely clever, and very cold. It could take the form of cynicism, or of despair.

In famous words Shakespeare once represented a form of this mood. Macbeth, now with many murders behind him, hears that his wife has died. Though she had been very close to him, he cannot feel what he would expect to feel. He answers the messenger:

> She should have died hereafter;
> There would have been a time for such a word.
> Tomorrow, and tomorrow, and tomorrow,
> Creeps in this petty pace from day to day,
> To the last syllable of recorded time;
> And all our yesterdays have lighted fools
> The way to dusty death. Out, out, brief candle!
> Life's but a walking shadow, a poor player
> That struts and frets his hour upon the stage,
> And then is heard no more; it is a tale
> Told by an idiot, full of sound and fury,
> Signifying nothing.[47]

For Macbeth there is no way to recover the meaning of time — at least no way that he can find, within the hours left to him before his death. In *The Winter's Tale*, Leontes after hearing of the death of his queen, does find the way, through years of prayer. It leads him to the mystery of resurrection. But in the tragedy of *Macbeth* it is another man whose humble search for the graces that become a king leads him to the sources of true order.

The elemental spirits receive their times and places from the spirits of day and month and year. We too need to know our times and places. Meditation and prayer have always to start out from something greater than ourselves; and when we have truly felt this greatness, it shows us when and where our task is, within the whole. Time and space are no longer empty for us, no longer a wild tale or a grey desert, but ready to receive the glory of God.

When we visit a holy place, for example an ancient stone circle or a medieval cathedral, we often find that it stands in relation to cosmic directions; perhaps the rising or setting of sun, moon or stars. For any particular place on earth, these directions slowly change; and so a temple becomes a solemn reminder of how short rhythms are placed within great rhythms, and how space is governed by time. We are led out to those ultimate directions marked by the stars, though these, too, slowly move. For our vision from the earth, the planets circle within the great wheel of the zodiac. We look out towards Leo, Scorpio, Aquarius and Taurus; and the directions of cosmic space these constellations mark speak to us of the vast ages of time through which our world has lived its earlier incarnations, and within which it is now living. Leo speaks to us of the cosmic sacrifice by the Thrones, from which fire had its birth. Though the world-direction of Scorpio may seem dark to us, it is from thence that the glory and fragrance of the Old Sun, the cosmic gift of the Spirits of Wisdom, stream towards us. And from Aquarius we can learn of the dreaming world of waters guided by the Spirits of Movement. When we look up at the mighty constellation of Taurus, and the delicate haze of the Pleiades, we can feel the source of that universe within which we now live, and have to awaken to the work expected from us. Thus the great ages of time have their encounter within the widths of space; the royal tent of God is spread out, within which each of us has room.

Our present century finds it very difficult to believe in any relationship between the outer universe and the inner life of the soul. And yet it is quite evident that our rhythm of sleeping and waking corresponds to the rotation of the earth. Within the great orientation of the universe we have the smaller earthly orientation of east and south and west and north, corresponding for the northern hemisphere to sunrise, noon, sunset and midnight. Our inner life of soul is placed within the rhythm of waking and sleeping. Where within our time of waking we put quiet minutes — minutes during which we try to free ourselves from the immediate pressure of present events — depends upon our own free decision; but it is not the same, to find such a time in the morning or in the evening, or in the middle of the day. In sleep we were in the spiritual world, but usually unconscious of it; in meditation we can seek it consciously. It makes a great difference, how long ago our sleep was, or how soon we will sleep again.

In the early morning the sun is ascending, but its light is still gentle. One of the profound fragments of Heraclitus says: 'The sun is every day new'. Truly, the sun that shines this morning has never shone before. At midday, the sun in the south commands the world; the visible light, the turmoil of the day, can make it hard for the inner light. Solzhenitsyn has said that hastiness and superficiality are the psychic disease of the twentieth century. To be unhurried, and to break through the surface of things, is most difficult at noon. By evening we have come a long way from the sunrise; the day's dust thickens the air. And yet like waggons from the harvest fields, human souls are beginning to carry back towards the spiritual world the achievements and discoveries of the day. At night our bodies may hinder us, when we try to complete this journey out into sleep. And yet, quietness can become easier, if we seek it.

In our meditation, three realms meet. We are helped in our seeking for quietness by the Third Hierarchy, and particularly by our own Angels. The great realm behind the visible radiance of the sun, the realm of the Second Hierarchy, streams then into the quietness. Beyond the wide kingdom of the sun are the stars, from which there work the powers of the First Hierarchy; but these are present too in the innermost depths of the soul. Each meditation, however brief and humble it may be, can begin with the contemplation of a truth; and all living truth wings its way upwards, from the Angel towards the heights of the Cherubim. Truth that grows warm becomes praise and prayer; it seeks then the ripening warmth of the Seraphim, to be taken up into their song. And prayer will always turn us back again, sustained by the strength of the Spirits of Will, to take up our places and our work on the earth.

Gradually it may become clearer to us why man, in dealing with material things, has so immense a responsibility; why matter has to be such a dangerous thing. Man is being trusted with powers which can be as destructive as the greatest heavenly spirits have been positive in their creation. This is one of the most far-reaching spiritual trials, not just of individual men, but of humanity as a whole.

8. The Divine Trinity

Among the often enigmatic words of Heraclitus there is a far-reaching saying: 'One thing, the only truly wise, does not and does consent to be called by the name of Zeus.' To describe what is divine, human words are constantly inadequate; how can we suppose that the beings of the heavenly worlds could consent to be described by us? In a dialogue very much concerned with the teachings of Heraclitus, *Cratylus*, Plato returns to this theme more than once; even the names which the Gods have for each other are different from the names we have for them. And yet the being who is beyond all names does call upon men to speak of him. Human speech would become a deserted realm if spiritual reality were to be left out. Our words must live in this tension; not only as something our minds recognize, but as the response of our whole being to a call which we can never answer completely. For the spirits of the hierarchies do not only speak with each other — they try to speak with us as well. 'He who has ears to hear, let him hear.' To ask ourselves why we do not hear and understand and answer is one of the first great tasks of self-knowledge. In St Matthew's Gospel, in the parable of the wedding feast, when the guests are at last assembled, one of them is questioned about his lack of a wedding garment. 'And he was speechless'.[48] The wedding is a meeting between the spiritual and the earthly. Each human being can feel himself in the position of unpreparedness for this meeting; the wedding garment is the soul filled with reverence and humility, prepared to reflect within it the colours and forms of the spiritual world.

A child learns to speak by listening, not only to the words spoken directly to it, but also to the conversations that go on around it. Some children show quite plainly that they expect a certain standard of themselves, before they are willing to speak — though to say this is to express a profound feeling in external, grown-up words. Others are reluctant to commit themselves at all to the dangerous sea of human speech. This may be found in an extreme form in some autistic children who may speak quite clearly and effectively when very much moved or astonished and then relapse into silence again for a long period. Similarly, human beings may find themselves suddenly able to pray when very much concerned about a beloved person, though at other times they may not even believe that prayer has any sense at all.

We have all listened to our elders, the spirits of the hierarchies — when we are asleep and before we were born. But if we have lost the necessary reverence from our souls, it may be difficult to recover any memory at all for this during waking life. But we do prepare ourselves by the way we practise listening in ordinary life. There are two ways of receiving sounds from the world around us. We may react with an instant liking or disliking, an immediate approval or disapproval of what we hear. Or we may give the sound time to unfold itself, as it were, within our own souls. The sounds of birds and animals, of natural events and machines, all become more significant for us if we have the patience to grow in sympathy and understanding towards them. It is particularly difficult not to become impatient when listening to other people's opinions; the impulse to correct them, almost before the words are out of their mouths, is very strong in most of us, it is even there in small children. A girl may tell her mother, within one brief discussion, not to speak so loudly, not to whisper, and not to be so silent. Later on we may come to the conclusion that almost everything said by everyone else is more or less nonsense. Our inner world has then become so noisy, so full of argument and complaint, that it becomes hardly possible to hear anything. This is what is called in the Gospels the realm of 'weeping and gnashing of teeth'. The way back from this realm into the light-filled banqueting hall, where the wedding feast is going on, is long, and yet short. The man who thinks everyone else is a fool could agree with Heraclitus in speaking of 'the only truly wise', though he identifies this with himself. But it is only a short step to see that *this* is not true. Even a worm in the soil has more wisdom in its organisms than our minds can contain.

When we develop a sense of humility towards the abundant wisdom which is hidden in everything around us, we also listen better to the opinions of other human beings who are our neighbours. We begin to observe that views which seem quite opposite may both be true. We may even reach the conclusion that everything said out of a desire to express the truth has a certain rightness about it. What men assert is generally true; it is when we reject or deny, or refuse to believe that there can be anything further to be said on some subject or other, that we go wrong. When a group of people are all prepared to listen to one another, believing in the contributions that each can bring, the presence of a heavenly power can be felt at work, the power which the Gospels, and in particular the Gospel of St John, describe as the Spirit of Truth, the Holy Spirit.

This power can be felt as active in what seem quite trivial matters. And yet it is a power greater than all the nine hierarchies, as this book has tried to indicate: part indeed of the divine Trinity. We should therefore be very much aware of the inadequacy of our words when we attempt to describe it, as we have tried to be with all the heavenly spirits. We can test each of the words that are used for writings which we hold in respect and see how relatively poor our understanding for them has become. 'Truth' is still a great word, but has often shrunk in men's minds to mean the exact correspondence between external events and a description of them. How far can we still give a real meaning to the word 'holy'? In the Greek New Testament there is a great word which is variously translated into English — *Paraklētos*, the Comforter or Advocate. It means literally the one called in, called to one's side — with the implicit sense that the one who calls is in some grave difficulty. Facing an accusation, or in bewilderment, or having lost the way, we may very much need an adviser. The Christ spoke of this to his disciples, particularly when he described their need in the future, when they would see him no longer. The Holy Spirit would help them to remember what he had said, and to learn what he had not yet been able to say to them; to answer their enemies, and to see the significance in a man's destiny of different kinds of fault and failure.

It was part of the guidance given by Rudolf Steiner to those who inaugurated The Christian Community that the Holy Spirit should be understood now and in the further future through the idea of healing. We can bring together — not in a trivial way, but in face of all the complexities of human destinies — the problems of human sickness and those of human sin, and see the Holy Spirit at work in all that is achieved as genuine healing. It is not for nothing that our faults and failures always in some way have their effect on those around us and call people together to help us, and to put right what has gone wrong for others as well. For example a man may have an accident, brought about by his own mistake in driving a car and suffer an injury for which he goes to hospital. From the moment of his mistake to the time of full recovery there may be hundreds of people who see him and think about his needs. And quite often there will be two or three people at a time, talking over what should be done, sometimes not only for his body, but for him as a person. The sense that these things go on constantly, and that the gentle wisdom at work in such consultations will increase through the centuries is one of the things that can most comfort us when we are anxious about the future.

When we share in concern about the needs of others, what happens in us can be compared to waking out of sleep. In the last dreams before morning, and perhaps in the first few minutes when we are aware of our bodies in bed, our consciousness is often limited to ourselves. As we come to full wakefulness, we become aware of what others are going to need of us during the coming day. But our picture of other people is in general very incomplete; often we find that people we meet in the course of the day, even some of those we regard as very near to us, are not at all in the state of mind we have supposed. We can come to realize that much of our lives is still spent in a kind of dream, even though we imagine ourselves to be awake. Looking into the future, whether we think of what is approaching us personally or of the future of mankind, we are looking towards greater wakefulness; a clearer and clearer awareness of the sufferings and joys, the moments of understanding and bewilderment, the impulses to action and the experiences of difficulty, through which other human beings and spiritual powers pass. It is in the light of the Holy Spirit that we shall awaken.

What Luke describes in the Acts of the Apostles as the event of Pentecost is a great example of this. Those who encounter the disciples in the streets of Jerusalem feel themselves addressed in the language of their own homes. For weeks the disciples have been absorbed in their meeting with the Risen Christ, and have in a sense turned away from the rest of humanity. Now the Holy Spirit illuminates for them all the people they encounter, in such a way that they see at once their questions and needs. And so the disciples can speak in a way that finds an immediate response. The power they had then will slowly develop in the future throughout the world. More and more people will feel in the very moment of speech how far their words are right and helpful for those who listen; and the light of the Holy Spirit will be felt to be just as real as, indeed more real than, the light of sun or stars, or any man-created light.

*   *   *

The New Testament is very sparing with the name of the Father-God. It is less sparing with the name of Christ; yet the name comes more seldom than we might expect, in a book of which he is after all the main theme. Throughout the

New Testament there is the strong sense that this name must only be used with deep reverence and humility, and at the right time. Quite often in the account of events for instance, the Gospels say 'he' where we might expect his name to be repeated for the sake of avoiding any ambiguity; and yet there is a great difference between the naming of the Father and the naming of the Son. With the naming of the Father the sense of the utter impossibility of describing him can never be far away; with the Son we are in the presence of the being in whom all naming has its source, who *is* Name. And if we look attentively we see that the New Testament abounds in great and fitting names for the Christ. None of them are used casually or just as alternatives; each must be approached with awe and a sense of the context in which it is to be used. But there is a fullness of names; and a feeling of their rightness can predominate for us over the sense — which of course must be there as well — of their incompleteness.

We can observe that the names vary, in that they may be more or less directly concerned with the Incarnation on earth. There are names which look more towards eternity, and others which are directly concerned with the sacrifice of Golgotha. 'Son' and 'Logos' are eternal names; 'Lamb of God' implies John the Baptist's foreknowledge of Golgotha. The name most often used by Christ of himself, 'Son of Man', contains the purpose of the Incarnation; and the sequence of wonderful names contained in St John's Gospel, beginning 'Bread of Life' and 'Light of the World' are all descriptions of the relationship of Christ to man.

The name 'Christ' is many-sided in its significance. It is the Greek word for 'anointed'. When in the ancient world a priest or a king was anointed, there was one who had the right to fulfil this act, in which the earthly substance, oil, was used to express the giving of grace to a human being whereby word and deed could be brought into harmony with the divine world. And there were those *for* whom he was anointed, his congregation or subjects. The words 'priest' and 'king' are themselves very seldom used in the New Testament as descriptions of Christ; the writer of the Letter to the Hebrews speaks of him as an eternal priest, to be compared with Melchizedek, rather than with the Hebrew priesthood. And the writer of the Apocalypse speaks of him as 'King of kings and Lord of lords'.[49] Those who follow him cannot truly be described as subjects (though they can be called servants); they are free and sovereign in themselves.

It is the Father by whom the Christ is anointed, that what is said and done by the Christ in all worlds may be in complete and unfailing harmony with the eternal purposes for which these worlds came into being. We have seen why oil, both in the Hebrew and Greek traditions, is used to express the power of bringing about harmonious and peaceful relationships and transitions; and that the olive tree gives to a landscape the quality of fostering this power. Paul brings his teaching in the first place to the whole Mediterranean region in which the olive flourishes so wonderfully. And in the Gospels there is one place which is singled out as having this quality. The Mount of Olives is the scene of certain great events. Here, looking across the Kildron valley to the eastern walls of Jerusalem and the Temple, Jesus speaks, two or three days before the Passion, to a small group of disciples about the future of the earth and his own return 'in the clouds'. And it is on the Mount of Olives, at what we call the Ascension, that he goes beyond the limits of his disciples' vision, uniting himself with the whole life of the earth. Later on, it is as Paul comes down form the barren heights to the olive terraces around Damascus that he beholds the Christ in vision.

The name Jesus is used in the New Testament in very close association with the name, Christ. It is a Hebrew personal name, 'God saves'. It is used for the earthly man, into whom the eternal Christ-spirit enters. Thus it can be said, 'Jesus of Nazareth'; and for St John the decisive work of the Christian is this recognition — that Jesus is the Christ. When the two names are put together the Incarnation and

Passion are being emphasized, the divine, suffering in man.

But it is one-sided, and indeed one of the weaknesses which has limited traditional Christianity, if we think of the work of Christ as concerned only with the redemption of man. He is there, and works, for all the hierarchies, for the elemental beings, and for all the creatures of earth. Just as man, looking towards the Christ-spirit can learn what it truly means to be a man, in the same way an angel or a member of another rank of the hierarchies learns afresh about his place in the universe through the contemplation of Christ's being and work. We can try to think of this quite concretely; an angel has in the present time to face in the development of mankind much that is deeply puzzling for him. The human being entrusted to his care is developing in directions that bring quite new tasks for the Angels. And when they turn towards the Christ they can see him in an angel-form, as has been briefly indicated earlier in this book, and see how he guides and comforts human beings as they face the bitter strangeness that seems to be coming over their world.

The elemental beings too are facing peculiar difficulties through the development of human technology. We are spoiling the places where they were so much at home — the wonderful hedges of England for example. In everything — air and sea, plant and animal — they meet the results of human intervention through which their tasks grow harder. They can be tempted, too, to abandon work that the earth needs. But if beings from among the elemental hosts are able to feel the presence of Christ, they are renewed and strengthened in their power to help the earth. A gnome understands better, so to speak, what it means to be a gnome, an undine what it means to be an undine. Here man can help through the way he looks at rocks and streams and through the fulfilment of sacraments in which the substances of earth are rightly used. Every human habitation can help or hinder the understanding of the elementals for the Deed of Christ.

Many, many new names we can hope to learn, when we grow to share these things more intimately. For things and beings have various names according to the standpoint from which they are seen.

In modern European languages there are certain words which are asked to express too wide a variety of meanings. Among these are the words which describe positive and warm relationships between human beings; such words for instance as 'love' and 'like' and 'be fond of'. It is a token of the state of a civilization that it gives a particular range of meanings to the word 'love' or its equivalents. The early Christians gave a great deal of new meaning to the Greek words they used, particularly to the word *agape*. The Middle Ages softened and deepened many Latin words. In our time there are many words that need to be raised again, often from the most trivial and distorted uses. We can perhaps say — if in any language the word 'Christ' is to be rightly used, there must be a word for love which can mean a selfless and devoted work for other beings. Just as we can consecrate things for definite purposes, so words need to be consecrated anew if they are to be companions for the divine names.

* * *

It has been said that the failure of human language is greatest when it tries to describe the Ground of the World, the Father. Yet the first petition of the basic Christian prayer is 'Hallowed be Thy Name'. In the wonderful structure of the Lord's Prayer we can distinguish the first three petitions from the last four. The first three look towards the whole future of mankind. They call for transformation of everything that man is and does — his understanding of the world, his society, his dealings with the kingdoms of nature. The last four petitions come nearer, though their implications are still very far-reaching. But we are reminded of the fact that we eat every day and that we have to be forgiven and to forgive almost every hour. To give meaning to the names of

121

God is something we achieve only very slowly. It is to this slow work that the word 'hallow' refers. The name of the Father cannot really be hallowed without the patient attempt to hallow every word and thought.

In the twentieth century we meet a peculiar difficulty in using the word 'Father'. For in countless earthly families the idea of the father's place and responsibility has been under a strain. How many men, particularly in Europe, looking back in later life, feel deep uncertainty and often even acute self-reproach, about the part they have played as fathers? Mothers indeed very often feel that they have been inadequate, but there is far more general agreement about the duty of a mother towards her children than about the duty of a father.

From childhood onwards we wrestle with the problem of freedom. We want to be free beings, but there is great difficulty in knowing what freedom is. We want to respect the freedom of others, but there are great difficulties in doing this, particularly within families. The earthly father of today is in a continual dilemma: 'If I tell my child what to do, I interfere with his freedom; if I do not tell him what to do, I neglect my duty and show myself indifferent.' The objection may well be made that earthly fathers are continually solving this dilemma by the use of common sense; and at a certain level this is of course true, but do many people, looking back, feel that their earthly fathers found a real and lasting solution, a real harmony between respect for their children's freedom and loving concern for what they experienced and did? Where moments of such harmony do light up in memory, we come near to the archetype of human fatherhood, and to the reason for its use as an analogy, though of course an infinitely imperfect analogy, for the relationship between creative beings and the Ground of the World.

Whenever Jesus uses the word 'Father', either speaking of the Ground of the World or of human relationships, the sense of this unity is not far away. A great example is the parable of the Prodigal Son. The father completely accepts his son's wish to take his share of the family's possessions and go far away and does not reproach him when he returns with nothing. A wonderful understanding is expressed in the gifts he makes to his son; a new robe, a ring, and shoes. And when the Prodigal's brother is angry, the father respects *his* freedom too; he does not command him to come but goes out and speaks with him gently.[1] (It is good to observe the delicate alternation between 'you' and 'we' in this passage.)

All that Christ Jesus says about the Father can contribute to our understanding; nearly all that theologians have said hinders this understanding because they have generally used a kind of thinking unfit for the grasping of spiritual realities. For example, it has often been said: suffering is imperfection; God is perfect; therefore God does not suffer. Those who accepted this argument did not see how radically they were contradicting the whole spirit of the New Testament. It is quite clear that the God who is concerned about the fall of a sparrow suffers with his creatures. And when Jesus tells his disciples that he is going to reveal the Father completely, he is preparing for the Passion.

Not very long ago it was comparatively rare for human beings to have a feeling for the suffering of animals. Rudolf Steiner sometimes directed our compassion upwards, for instance in his description in letters written during his last illness, of the suffering endured by the Archangel Michael in preparation for his mission which would begin in 1879; his anxiety for humanity. Human beings in our time can make the first beginnings in compassion not only for the creatures of earth but for heavenly powers.

We think of the ground beneath our feet as something passive, trodden down by us. But it is also possible to think of it as active — as carrying us, sustaining us. When the divine Father is described as Ground of the World, the active bearing and sustaining of all beings is meant, in whatever world they may be. When we leave this earth which has sustained us, we tread another ground, but the spiritual being who holds us is the same and this holding not only gives us a place to be, but actively blesses us, wills us to be what we are in our innermost nature. Just as the Prodigal Son is sustained throughout his journey and through his meaningless deeds by what he has received as inheritance, so the Father sustains beings who for part of their existence oppose the will which has created them. But as all come from him, so all return; humble, richer in experience, and filled with joy as they draw near.

References

1. Shakespeare, *Twelfth Night*, V,i
2. Shakespeare, *Troilus & Cressida*, I,iii
3. Shakespeare, *Sonnet 29*
4. Shakespeare, *Henry V*, IV,i
5. John 8:32
6. A.Carmichael, *Carmina Gadelica*, Vol.I, p.49
7. Shakespeare, *Sonnet 18*
8. Shakespeare, *Sonnet 98*
9. Shakespeare, *Macbeth*, IV,iii
10. Wolfram von Eschenbach, *Parzival*, Book V, §252
11. Shakespeare, *Cymbeline*, IV,ii
12. Jude 9
13. Rev.11:8
14. Rev.12:7-12
15. Tobit 12:15
16. A.Carmichael, *Carmina Gadelica*, Vol.I, p.89-91
17. A.Carmichael, *Carmina Gadelica*, Vol.I, p.305
18. John 12:31
19. *Kalevala*, Runo VIII, 1.271ff
20. Gen.1:3
21. Gen.18
22. Gen.2:5
23. Exod.3:14
24. Luke 24:39
25. Rev.1:17-18
26. John 20:22
27. Gen.2:7
28. Shakespeare, *Pericles*, III,i
29. Matt.26:64
30. Matt.24:29
31. Gen.14:18-20
32. Gen.4:2-5
33. Heb.7:3
34. John 14:27
35. Matt.5:48
36. Rev.4:2
37. Isa.6:1
38. Rev.3:21
39. Rev.4:3
40. Rev.17:4
41. J. Colet, *Celestial Hierarchy*, (in *Two Treatises on the Hierarchies of Dionysius*, Ed. Lupton, London 1869)
42. Rev.22:15
43. Gen.3:24
44. Isa.6:6-8
45. Shakespeare, *King Lear*, V,ii
46. Ezek.1:17-21
47. Shakespeare, *Macbeth*, V,v
48. Matt.22:12
49. Rev.19:16